The Basics *of* Nichiren Buddhism

The Basics *of* Nichiren Buddhism

World Tribune Press

SGI-USA Introductory and Intermediate Exam Study Material

Published by World Tribune Press
A division of the SGI-USA
606 Wilshire Blvd., Santa Monica, CA 90401

Printed in the United States of America.

Cover and interior design by Jocelyn Hsu.

28 27 26 25 24 1 2 3 4 5

ISBN: 978-1-944604-97-4 (paperback)

Contents

Part 2: Material for Both the Introductory Exam and the Intermediate Exam

Part 3: Material for the Intermediate Exam

Editor's Note

GZ, page number(s)—refers to the *Gosho zenshu*, the Japanese-language compilation of letters, treatises, essays, and oral teachings of Nichiren Daishonin.

LSOC, page number(s)—refers to *The Lotus Sutra and Its Opening and Closing Sutras*, translated by Burton Watson (Soka Gakkai: Tokyo, 2009).

OTT, page number(s)—refers to *The Record of the Orally Transmitted Teachings*, translated by Burton Watson (Soka Gakkai: Tokyo, 2004).

WND, page number(s)—refers to *The Writings of Nichiren Daishonin*, vol. 1 (WND-1) (Tokyo: Soka Gakkai, 1999) and vol. 2 (WND-2) (Tokyo: Soka Gakkai, 2006).

References to dates in *The Writings of Nichiren Daishonin* are from the lunisolar calendar that was used in thirteenth-century Japan, which differs from the current Gregorian calendar commonly used in the West.

Preface

Studying Buddhism and embracing its empowering concepts help us develop our faith and establish a regular daily practice. Studying a little every day is ideal. We often learn about Buddhist principles and topics at our monthly discussion, study, and divisional meetings, as well as at other SGI activities.

Working toward SGI-USA study exams also helps us deepen our understanding of Buddhism. Every year, members and guests have the opportunity to take the Introductory Exam. After passing this first exam, members can take the Intermediate Exam.

This booklet contains material for both exams: part 1 covers material for the Introductory Exam, part 2 is for both the Introductory and Intermediate Exams, and part 3 for the Intermediate Exam. With the exceptions of chapters 11 and 18, the material in this booklet is from "The Basics of Nichiren Buddhism for the New Era of Worldwide Kosen-rufu," published on SokaGlobal.org (https://tinyurl.com/SGIstudy).

Additional exam material may be published in the *World Tribune* and *Living Buddhism* before each exam, alongside sample questions and other tools.

For some people, the thought of taking an exam can be daunting or a cause for stress and anxiety. But rather than emphasizing passing these exams, SGI exams drive home the importance of study, a vital aspect of Buddhist practice for understanding our lives and circumstances from the enlightened Buddhist perspective. Studying Buddhism helps us effect change in our personal lives and within our families, workplaces, and communities. It also helps us more confidently share Buddhism with others. Ikeda Sensei adds:

> Earnest study of the Daishonin's writings gives momentum to our movement for kosen-rufu and is the key to the solid foundation of the Soka Gakkai's people-centered organization. It is also the driving force for fostering capable individuals and promoting dynamic development for an eternally youthful Soka Gakkai.[1]

Whether new to Buddhism or a longtime practitioner, we hope this booklet serves as a tool for gaining a better understanding of Buddhist perspectives on the workings of life and applying them to all aspects of life.

NOTE:

1. *World Tribune*, February 25, 2011, 4.

The Purpose of Studying Buddhism

The following is an excerpt from Ikeda Sensei's monthly message titled "Shining Our Light as Bodhisattvas of the Earth for the Happiness of the People," published in the October 2023 Living Buddhism.

"**Exert yourself in** the two ways of practice and study" ("The True Aspect of All Phenomena," WND-1, 386)—this is one of the eternal guidelines of the Soka Gakkai.

How highly Nichiren Daishonin, the Buddha of the Latter Day of the Law, would praise the noble efforts of all of you, my friends around the world, who are preparing for Buddhist study exams or participating in study courses with eager seeking spirit.

All that you are learning as you study Nichiren Buddhism together with fellow members—each of you taking time out of your busy schedules while dealing with all kinds of personal challenges—will be engraved deeply in your lives and become a source of immense joy, good fortune, and benefit.

In September 1950, when I was working frantically to transform the dire situation of the businesses of my mentor, Josei Toda, I copied a passage from "Medicine King," the twenty-third chapter of the Lotus Sutra, in my diary: "This sutra can cause all living beings to free themselves from suffering and anguish. This sutra can bring great benefits to all living beings and fulfill their desires" (LSOC, 327–28). These words are a declaration that the Mystic Law is the supreme and ultimate teaching for relieving the sufferings of all living beings.

I felt as if I could hear the loud voice that issued from the magnificent assembly of the Lotus Sutra calling out: "You must spread [the Lotus Sutra] abroad widely throughout Jambudvipa [the entire world] and never allow it to be cut off" (LSOC, 330).

Retreating was not an option. I resolved to support my mentor, who was leading the propagation of the great Law, and first do everything I could to break through the immediate obstacles that stood in our path.

As Soka Gakkai members, we read Nichiren Daishonin's writings and the Lotus Sutra, and chant Nam-myoho-renge-kyo for the happiness of ourselves and others. We base our lives on the ultimate truth of the universe. When we view our problems from the vast perspective of life encompassing past, present, and future and the worlds of the ten directions, what incredible courage and wisdom and powerful life force well up within us to embrace and overcome them!

The Daishonin writes in "The Entity of the Mystic Law," which he composed 750 years ago [in 1273] while in exile on Sado Island, that Myoho-renge is the "wonderful single Law [*myoho*] that simultaneously possesses both cause and effect [*renge*]" and that "anyone who practices this Law will obtain both the cause and the effect of Buddhahood simultaneously" (WND-1, 421). How profound "the cause and effect of Buddhahood" we obtain through exerting ourselves tirelessly in the "two ways of practice and study," undaunted by all difficulties!

Part 1: Material for the Introductory Exam

CHAPTER 1

The Life of Nichiren Daishonin

Nichiren Daishonin (1222–82) dedicated his life to propagating the Mystic Law—Nam-myoho-renge-kyo—motivated by an unwavering commitment and compassion to eradicate suffering and enable all people to reveal their innate Buddhahood. He encountered unrelenting hardship and persecution throughout his life as he sought to address and put an end to the evils obstructing the happiness of the people.

Early Years

The Daishonin was born on February 16, 1222,[1] in the coastal hamlet of Kataumi in Tojo Village of Nagasa District in Awa Province (part of present-day Kamogawa City in Chiba Prefecture). He was the son of commoners, his family earning its livelihood from fishing.

At the age of twelve, he began his schooling at a nearby temple called Seicho-ji. During this period, he made a vow to become the wisest person in Japan (see "The Tripitaka Master Shan-wu-wei," WND-1, 175). He sought to gain the wisdom of the Buddhist teachings for overcoming the fundamental sufferings of life and death and thereby lead his parents and all people to genuine happiness.

At sixteen, in pursuit of a deeper understanding of the Buddhist teachings, he formally entered the priesthood at Seicho-ji, receiving instruction from Dozen-bo, a senior priest there. It was shortly thereafter, the Daishonin writes, that he attained "a jewel of wisdom as bright as the morning star" (WND-1, 176). This can be interpreted to mean wisdom regarding the Mystic Law that is the essence of Buddhism.

The Daishonin then traveled to Kamakura, Kyoto, Nara, and other centers of Buddhist learning, carefully studying the sutras and commentaries housed at leading temples such as Enryaku-ji on Mount Hiei, the headquarters of the Tendai school, and familiarizing himself with the core doctrines of each school. He confirmed that the Lotus Sutra is the foremost among all the Buddhist sutras and that the Law of Nam-myoho-renge-kyo to which he had awakened is the essence of the sutra and provides the means for freeing all people from suffering on the most fundamental level. He also awoke to his mission to spread Nam-myoho-renge-kyo as the teaching for people in the Latter Day of the Law[2] to attain enlightenment.

The Declaration of the Establishment of His Teaching

Through his studies at leading Buddhist centers, the Daishonin confirmed his mission to spread the Mystic Law—Nam-myoho-renge-kyo—and the means by which to do so. He embarked on his struggle knowing that he would inevitably encounter great opposition and persecution.

On April 28, 1253, around noon at Seicho-ji, he refuted the Nembutsu and other Buddhist teachings of his day as erroneous and proclaimed Nam-myoho-renge-kyo to be the sole correct Buddhist teaching for leading all people in the Latter Day of the Law to enlightenment. This is known as the declaration of the establishment of his teaching. He was thirty-two years old. From around this time, he adopted the name Nichiren (literally, sun lotus).

The Daishonin's denunciation of the Nembutsu doctrines on the occasion of declaring his teaching enraged Tojo Kagenobu, who was the local steward (an official of the Kamakura government who had the powers of law enforcement and tax collection) and an ardent Nembutsu believer. Kagenobu planned an armed attack on the Daishonin, but the Daishonin narrowly managed to escape beforehand.

The Daishonin then made his way to Kamakura, the seat of the military government. There, he took up residence in a small dwelling in Nagoe (at a site that later came to be known as Matsubagayatsu) and embarked in earnest on propagating his teaching. While refuting the error of the Nembutsu and Zen teachings, which had gained wide influence among the people of Kamakura, the Daishonin spread the teaching of Nam-myoho-renge-kyo.

It was during this early period of propagation that such well-known disciples as Toki Jonin, Shijo Kingo (Shijo Yorimoto), and Ikegami Munenaka (the elder of the Ikegami brothers) converted to his teaching.

Submitting the Treatise "On Establishing the Correct Teaching for the Peace of the Land" and Encountering Persecution

In the period when the Daishonin began his propagation efforts in Kamakura, Japan had been experiencing a series of natural disasters and calamities, including extreme weather, severe earthquakes, famine, fires, and epidemics. In particular, the devastating earthquake of the Shoka era, which struck the Kamakura region in August 1257, destroyed many homes and important buildings in Kamakura.

This disaster prompted the Daishonin to write the treatise "On Establishing the Correct Teaching for the Peace of the Land" (see WND-1, 6–26) to clarify the fundamental cause of people's suffering and set forth the means by which people could eradicate such suffering. On July 16, 1260, he submitted this treatise to Hojo Tokiyori, the retired regent of the Kamakura military government who was still effectively the country's most powerful leader. It was the first time that the Daishonin remonstrated with the authorities. This is known as his first remonstration with the government authorities.

In this treatise, he declared that the cause of the successive calamities lay with people's slander of the correct teaching of Buddhism and their reliance on erroneous doctrines. The most serious root cause, he asserted, was the Nembutsu teaching popularized in Japan by the priest Honen.

The Daishonin urged people to discontinue their reliance on such erroneous teachings and embrace faith in the correct teaching of Buddhism without delay, for this would ensure the realization of a peaceful and prosperous land. Continued reliance on erroneous teachings, he warned, would inevitably result in the country encountering internal strife and foreign invasion—the two calamities of the three calamities and seven disasters[3] yet to occur.

However, the ruling authorities ignored the Daishonin's sincere remonstration and, with their tacit approval, Nembutsu followers began plotting to persecute the Daishonin.

One evening shortly after the Daishonin submitted his treatise "On Establishing the Correct Teaching for the Peace of the Land," a group of Nembutsu believers stormed his dwelling in an attempt to take his life. This is called the Matsubagayatsu Persecution. However, the Daishonin escaped unharmed. After this incident, he left Kamakura for a short period.

On May 12, 1261, the following year, having returned to Kamakura sometime earlier, the Daishonin was arrested by the authorities and sentenced to exile in Ito in Izu Province. This is called the Izu Exile. After being pardoned from exile in February 1263, the Daishonin made his way back to Kamakura.

In 1264, he returned to his home province of Awa to visit his ailing mother. On November 11 of that year, the Daishonin and a group of his followers were on their way to the residence of another follower named Kudo in Amatsu (also in Awa Province). At a place called Matsubara in Tojo Village, they were ambushed by a band of armed men under the command of the local steward, Tojo Kagenobu. In the attack, the Daishonin sustained an injury to his forehead and a broken left hand. One of his followers was killed at the site. This is called the Komatsubara Persecution.

The Tatsunokuchi Persecution and Casting Off the Transient and Revealing the True

In 1268, an official letter arrived in Kamakura from the Mongol Empire demanding that Japan become one of its tributaries and threatening military attack should the demand be rejected. With this development, the danger of the calamity of foreign invasion befalling the nation became very real.

This spurred the Daishonin to write eleven letters of remonstration to top government officials, including Regent Hojo Tokimune, and the heads of major Buddhist temples in Kamakura. In the letters, he stated that the impending danger of an invasion was just as he had predicted in his treatise "On Establishing the Correct Teaching for the Peace of the Land," and he expressed the hope that the priests of the various Buddhist schools would meet with him in an official public debate.

Neither the government leaders nor the religious establishment heeded the Daishonin's appeal. Rather, viewing the Daishonin's community of believers as a threat to the existing power structure, the government began to take repressive measures against it.

Around this time, True Word priests were enjoying growing influence, the government having charged them with the mission of conducting prayers for the defeat of Mongol forces. Ryokan (also known as Ninsho) of Gokuraku-ji temple in Kamakura, a priest of the True Word Precepts school, was also becoming more influential through his connections with powerful government figures.

The Daishonin fearlessly began to refute the errors of the established Buddhist schools that were exerting a negative influence on the people and society as a whole.

In the summer of 1271, in response to a prolonged drought, the government ordered Ryokan to pray for rain. Learning of this, the Daishonin made a proposal to Ryokan: if Ryokan should succeed in producing rain within seven days, the Daishonin would become his disciple; but if he failed to do so, then Ryokan should place his faith in the Lotus Sutra.

When his prayers failed to produce any rain after seven days had passed, Ryokan asked for a seven-day extension. Again no rain fell, but fierce gales arose instead. Ryokan had clearly lost the challenge.

Rather than honestly acknowledge defeat, however, Ryokan grew even more hostile toward the Daishonin. He contrived to bring accusations against the Daishonin by filing a false complaint with the government in the name of a Nembutsu priest Ryokan had close ties with. He also used his influence with top government officials as well as their wives to have the Daishonin persecuted by the authorities.

Although Ryokan was widely respected among the populace as a devout and virtuous priest, he enjoyed the trappings of power and privilege and colluded with government officials toward self-serving ends.

On September 10 of the same year (1271), the Daishonin was summoned by the government and interrogated by Hei no

Saemon-no-jo Yoritsuna (also known as Taira no Yoritsuna), the deputy chief of the Office of Military and Police Affairs (the chief being the regent himself). The Daishonin admonished him and emphasized the proper attitude for the nation's rulers based on the correct teaching of Buddhism.

Two days later, on September 12, Hei no Saemon-no-jo, leading a group of armed soldiers, raided the Daishonin's dwelling and arrested him, treating him as if he were a traitor. On that occasion, strongly remonstrating with Hei no Saemon-no-jo, the Daishonin stated that in persecuting him they had "just toppled the pillar of Japan" ("The Actions of the Votary of the Lotus Sutra," WND-1, 766) and warned that this would cause the calamities of internal strife and foreign invasion to descend on the land. The events on September 10 and 12 marked his second remonstration with the government authorities.

Late that night, the Daishonin was suddenly taken by armed soldiers to the beach at Tatsunokuchi on the outskirts of Kamakura. This was at the directive of Hei no Saemon-no-jo and others who conspired to have the Daishonin secretly beheaded there. Just as the executioner raised his sword to strike, however, a brilliant orb of light burst forth from the direction of the nearby island of Enoshima, shooting northwest across the sky. The soldiers were terrified, and the attempt to kill the Daishonin had to be abandoned. This is called the Tatsunokuchi Persecution.

This persecution had extremely important significance for the Daishonin. In triumphing over the Tatsunokuchi Persecution, he cast off his transient status as an ordinary, unenlightened person burdened with karma and suffering and, while remaining an ordinary human being, revealed his original, true identity as a Buddha possessing infinite wisdom and compassion (the Buddha of beginningless time or eternal Buddha). This is called casting off the transient and revealing the true.

Thereafter, the Daishonin's behavior was that of the Buddha of the Latter Day of the Law, and he went on to inscribe the Gohonzon for all people to revere and embrace as the fundamental object of devotion.

The Sado Exile

While the government was deliberating on his fate following the Tatsunokuchi Persecution, the Daishonin was housed for about a month at the residence of Homma Shigetsura (the deputy provincial military governor of Sado) in Echi, Sagami Province (part of present-day Atsugi City, Kanagawa Prefecture). During this period, the Daishonin's followers in Kamakura were subjected to many forms of persecution, including being unjustly accused of arson, murder, and other crimes.

Eventually, the Daishonin was sentenced to exile on Sado Island (part of present-day Niigata Prefecture). He departed from Echi on October 10, arriving at the graveyard of Tsukahara on Sado on November 1. The dwelling he was assigned there was a small, dilapidated hut called the Sammaido, which had been used for funerary rites. The conditions the Daishonin faced were truly harsh. It was bitterly cold on Sado, and he lacked sufficient food and warm clothing. In addition, he was surrounded by hostile Nembutsu followers who sought to take his life.

The Daishonin's followers in Kamakura also continued to suffer persecution. Some were even imprisoned or banished or had their lands confiscated. The majority of his remaining followers began to have doubts and discarded their faith out of fear and a desire for self-preservation.

On January 16 and 17, 1272, several hundred Buddhist priests from Sado and nearby provinces on the mainland gathered at Tsukahara with the intent to kill the Daishonin. They were stopped by Homma Shigetsura, who proposed that they engage the Daishonin in a religious debate instead. In the debate that ensued, the Daishonin thoroughly refuted the erroneous teachings of the various Buddhist schools of his day. This is known as the Tsukahara Debate.

In February, a faction of the ruling Hojo clan rose up in rebellion, and fighting broke out in Kamakura and Kyoto, the seat of the military government and imperial capital, respectively. This is known as the Disturbance of the Second Month or the Hojo Tokisuke Rebellion. The Daishonin's prediction of internal strife had come true just 150 days after declaring it in his remonstration with Hei no Saemon-no-jo at the time of the Tatsunokuchi Persecution.

In early summer of that year, the Daishonin was transferred from Tsukahara to Ichinosawa, also on Sado, but his life continued to be threatened by angry Nembutsu followers.

During the Sado Exile, Nikko Shonin, who later became the Daishonin's successor, faithfully followed and served him and shared his sufferings. The Daishonin also steadily gained followers while on Sado Island, including Abutsu-bo and his wife, the lay nun Sennichi.

The Daishonin composed many important works during his exile on Sado. Of special significance are "The Opening of the Eyes" and "The Object of Devotion for Observing the Mind."

"The Opening of the Eyes," written in February 1272, explains that the Daishonin is the votary of the Lotus Sutra of the Latter Day of the Law who is practicing in exact accord with the teachings of the Lotus Sutra. Ultimately, it reveals his identity as the Buddha of the Latter Day of the Law endowed with the three virtues of sovereign, teacher, and parent to lead all people in the latter age to enlightenment.

"The Object of Devotion for Observing the Mind," completed in April 1273, presents the object of devotion of Nam-myoho-renge-kyo to be embraced by all people in the Latter Day of the Law in order to attain Buddhahood.

In February 1274, the Daishonin was pardoned, and in March he departed from Sado and returned to Kamakura.

Meeting Hei no Saemon-no-jo in April, the Daishonin strongly remonstrated with him, denouncing the government's actions in ordering priests to pray for the defeat of the Mongols based on the True Word and other erroneous Buddhist teachings. Further, responding to a direct question from Hei no Saemon-no-jo, he predicted that the Mongol invasion would most certainly take place before the year's end. This marked his third remonstration with the government authorities.

Just as the Daishonin predicted, a large Mongol fleet attacked Kyushu, the westernmost of Japan's four main islands, in October 1274. This is referred to as the first Mongol invasion.

With this event, the two predictions he had made in "On Establishing the Correct Teaching for the Peace of the Land"—those of internal strife and foreign invasion—had come true.

This was the third time that the Daishonin had directly remonstrated with the government authorities and predicted that disasters would befall the country. Affirming that his predictions had been fulfilled, the Daishonin wrote, "Three times now I have gained distinction by having such knowledge" ("The Selection of the Time," WND-1, 579).

Taking Up Residence at Mount Minobu

When the government rejected his final remonstration, the Daishonin decided to leave Kamakura and take up residence in Hakii Village on the slopes of Mount Minobu in Kai Province (present-day Yamanashi Prefecture). The local steward was Hakii Sanenaga, who had become a follower of the Daishonin through the propagation efforts of Nikko Shonin.

The Daishonin moved to Mount Minobu in May 1274. His

change of residence, however, was by no means a retreat from the world.

He composed many of his major works there, including "The Selection of the Time" and "On Repaying Debts of Gratitude." In these writings, he elucidated numerous important teachings—in particular, the Three Great Secret Laws.[4]

Through lectures on the Lotus Sutra, he devoted himself to fostering disciples who would carry out kosen-rufu—broadly teaching and spreading the Mystic Law to realize peace and happiness for all people—in the future.

During this period, he also wrote many letters to his lay followers throughout the country, patiently instructing and encouraging them so they could persevere with strong faith, win in life, and attain the state of Buddhahood.

The Atsuhara Persecution and the Purpose of the Daishonin's Appearance in This World

After the Daishonin moved to Mount Minobu, Nikko Shonin actively led propagation efforts in the Fuji area of Suruga Province (present-day central Shizuoka Prefecture), successfully convincing many Tendai priests and followers to abandon their old religious affiliations and begin practicing the Daishonin's teaching.

This prompted harassment and persecution by local Tendai temples, and threats were directed at those who had embraced the Daishonin's teaching.

On September 21, 1279, twenty farmers who were followers of the Daishonin in Atsuhara, a village in Suruga Province, were arrested on trumped-up charges and taken to Kamakura. At the residence of Hei no Saemon-no-jo, they were subjected to harsh interrogation equivalent to torture. Though they were pressed to abandon their faith in the Lotus Sutra, they all remained true to their beliefs.

Three of the twenty followers arrested—the brothers Jinshiro, Yagoro, and Yarokuro—were ultimately executed, while the remaining seventeen were banished from their places of residence. This series of events is known as the Atsuhara Persecution.

The example of these farmers persevering in faith without begrudging their lives convinced the Daishonin that humble, ordinary people without any position in society had developed sufficiently strong faith to withstand great persecutions. In "On Persecutions Befalling the Sage," dated October 1, 1279, in the twenty-seventh year after proclaiming his teaching, he refers to the purpose of his appearance in this world (see "On Persecutions Befalling the Sage," WND-1, 996).

While still little more than a child, the Daishonin had vowed to become a person of wisdom who understood the essence of Buddhism and to free all people from suffering at the most fundamental level. The fulfillment of that vow was his life's guiding purpose. Expounding the teaching of Nam-myoho-renge-kyo, the fundamental Law for the enlightenment of all people, and revealing the Three Great Secret Laws, he established the foundation for kosen-rufu that would endure for all time.

During the Atsuhara Persecution, ordinary people who embraced faith in Nam-myoho-renge-kyo that encompasses the Three Great Secret Laws, dedicated themselves to kosen-rufu without begrudging their lives. Their appearance demonstrated that the Buddhism of Nichiren Daishonin was a teaching that would be championed by ordinary people, a teaching for the enlightenment of all humanity. The Daishonin thus fulfilled the purpose of his appearance in this world.

At the time of the Atsuhara Persecution, the Daishonin's followers strove in faith with the united spirit of many in body, one in mind. His youthful disciple Nanjo Tokimitsu, steward of a village neighboring Atsuhara, worked tirelessly to protect his fellow believers.

The Daishonin's Death and Nikko Shonin's Succession

On September 8, 1282, the Daishonin, who was in declining health, left Minobu, where he had resided for nine years. He departed with the stated intent of visiting the therapeutic hot springs in Hitachi Province (part of present-day Ibaraki and Fukushima Prefectures) at the recommendation of his disciples. When he arrived at the residence of his follower Ikegami Munenaka (the elder of the Ikegami brothers) in Ikegami in Musashi Province (present-day Ota Ward, Tokyo), he began to make arrangements for after his death.

On September 25, in spite of being gravely ill, he is said to have given a lecture to his followers on his treatise "On Establishing the Correct Teaching for the Peace of the Land."

The Daishonin passed away at Ikegami Munenaka's residence on October 13, 1282, at the age of sixty-one, bringing to a close his noble life as the votary of the Lotus Sutra.

After the Daishonin's death, only Nikko Shonin carried on his mentor's fearless spirit and actions for kosen-rufu. Based on his awareness as the Daishonin's successor, Nikko Shonin continued to speak out against slander of the Law and to remonstrate with the government authorities. He treasured every one of the Daishonin's writings, referring to them as honorable writings (Jpn *gosho*), and encouraged all disciples to read and study them as the sacred scripture for the Latter Day of the Law. He also fostered many outstanding disciples who exerted themselves in Buddhist practice and study.

NOTES:

1. Here, February 16, 1222, indicates the sixteenth day of the second month of 1222 on the lunar calendar, which was used for the purpose of recording dates during premodern times through the 1800s in countries such as Japan and China. The same approach is followed for other premodern dates that appear throughout the text.

2. The Latter Day of the Law refers to the age when the teachings of Shakyamuni Buddha lose their power to lead people to enlightenment. It was generally regarded to mean the period starting two thousand years after the Buddha's passing. In Japan, it was believed that this age began in the year 1052.

3. The three calamities and seven disasters are described in various sutras and differ slightly depending on the source. The three calamities include high grain prices or inflation (especially that caused by famine), warfare, and pestilence. The seven disasters include natural disasters such as extraordinary changes of the stars and planets and unseasonable storms.

4. The Three Great Secret Laws are core principles of Nichiren Daishonin's teachings. They are the object of devotion of the essential teaching (the Gohonzon), the daimoku of the essential teaching (Nam-myoho-renge-kyo), and the sanctuary of the essential teaching (where the Gohonzon is enshrined). They are called secret because they are implicit in the text of the "Life Span" chapter of the Lotus Sutra.

CHAPTER

2

Nam-myoho-renge-kyo

Nam-myoho-renge-kyo is the essence of Buddhism and the fundamental Law perceived by Nichiren Daishonin for resolving the suffering of all humanity. Here, we will examine a few of the important aspects of Nam-myoho-renge-kyo.

The Fundamental Law That Pervades the Universe and Life

Nam-myoho-renge-kyo is the fundamental Law that pervades the entire universe and all life.

Shakyamuni, the founder of Buddhism, viewed the sufferings of all people as his own and searched for a way to resolve those sufferings. In the process, he awakened to the truth that the eternal, all-pervading, fundamental Law of the universe and life existed within his own being. This realization led to his being known as Buddha, or awakened one. Then, with wisdom and compassion, he expounded numerous teachings, which later were compiled as Buddhist sutras. Among them, the Lotus Sutra teaches the true essence of the Buddha's enlightenment.

Nichiren Daishonin identified this Law to which Shakyamuni awakened—the Law that can resolve human suffering on a fundamental level and open the way to genuine happiness—as Nam-myoho-renge-kyo.

The Essential Law for Attaining Buddhahood

Buddhas are those who have embodied the Law in their own lives, overcome all suffering, and established an unshakable inner state of absolute happiness.

The Law of Nam-myoho-renge-kyo is the essential principle, or means, for attaining Buddhahood.

The Eternal Law Inherent in All People's Lives

Buddhas are awakened to the truth that the Law exists within not only their own lives but also the lives of all people. They realize that this all-pervasive Law transcends the bounds of life and death and can never be lost or destroyed.

The Law of Nam-myoho-renge-kyo is universal, inherent in all people; it is also eternal, persisting throughout the three existences of past, present, and future.

The Profound Meaning Reflected in the Name Nam-myoho-renge-kyo

The profound meaning of the fundamental Law is reflected in its name, Nam-myoho-renge-kyo.

Myoho-renge-kyo is the full title of the Lotus Sutra in Japanese and translates as "the Lotus Sutra of the wonderful (mystic) law."

Because the Law expounded in the Lotus Sutra is difficult to fathom and comprehend, it is called the Mystic Law (*myoho*).

The lotus (*renge*) is used as a metaphor to describe the distinctive characteristics of the Mystic Law.

Though it grows in muddy water, the lotus remains unsullied by its environment, producing pure and fragrant blooms. This conjures images of those who have faith in and practice the Mystic Law. Though they live in the real world that is rife with suffering, they remain pure in thought and action, teaching others and guiding them to enlightenment.

In addition, the lotus, unlike other plants, contains a seed pod (the lotus fruit) within its buds, and the flower and fruit grow and appear at the same time. The flower (the cause) and the fruit (the effect) exist together, simultaneously. This is also used to illustrate that the state of Buddhahood, though indiscernible, exists even in the lives of ordinary people who have not yet manifested that state of life and, further, that even after one becomes a Buddha, one does not lose the life states that characterize an ordinary person.

Kyo, meaning sutra, indicates that the Lotus Sutra (Myoho-renge-kyo) contains the eternal truth—the Mystic Law—and that people should venerate and place their faith in it.

Nam, or *namu*, is the phonetic rendering in Chinese characters of the Sanskrit word *namas*, meaning bow or reverence. This term was also translated using the Chinese characters meaning to dedicate one's life (*kimyo*). To dedicate one's life, in this sense, means to devote oneself body and mind to the Law and strive to practice and embody it with one's entire being.

Nam-myoho-renge-kyo is the very heart and essence of the Buddha, which is expressed in wise and compassionate action to lead all people to enlightenment.

Nichiren Daishonin's Enlightened State of Life

Although the Lotus Sutra teaches the fundamental Law of the universe and life, it does not reveal the exact nature or name of the Law.

Nichiren Daishonin awakened to the truth that the Law expounded in the Lotus Sutra existed in his own life, and he revealed that Law to be Nam-myoho-renge-kyo.

In other words, Nam-myoho-renge-kyo is not simply Myoho-renge-kyo, the title of the Lotus Sutra, prefaced by the word *nam*, but the name of the Law itself.

By revealing the Law to be Nam-myoho-renge-kyo, the Daishonin opened the way in real terms for fundamentally freeing people from suffering and delusion, which arise from ignorance of the true nature of their lives, and helping them build unshakable happiness.

That is why we revere Nichiren Daishonin as the Buddha of the Latter Day of the Law, an age filled with confusion and suffering.

Nam-myoho-renge-kyo is the enlightened life state of Buddhahood, or true identity, of the Daishonin, who embodied in his being the Law that pervades the universe and all existence.

Ordinary People Are Themselves the Mystic Law

The life state of Buddhahood is also inherent in the lives of unenlightened ordinary people—in every person. All people are inherently and originally Nam-myoho-renge-kyo itself.

However, while ignorant of this truth, ordinary people are unable to demonstrate the power and functions of the Law of Nam-myoho-renge-kyo that exist within them. To be awakened to this truth is the life state of a Buddha; to doubt or be unaware of this truth is the life state of one who is unenlightened. When we have faith in and actually practice Nam-myoho-renge-kyo, the power and functions of the Mystic Law are activated and expressed in our lives, and in this way we manifest the life state of Buddhahood.

The Object of Devotion for Practice, Revealed in the Form of a Mandala

Nichiren Daishonin depicted his own Buddhahood, or enlightened life state, in the form of a mandala. He made this the object of devotion (Jpn *gohonzon*) for our Buddhist practice so that we ordinary people can manifest Nam-myoho-renge-kyo in our lives and attain Buddhahood, just as he did.

The Daishonin writes: "Never seek this Gohonzon outside yourself. The Gohonzon exists only within the mortal flesh of us ordinary people who embrace the Lotus Sutra and chant Nam-myoho-renge-kyo" ("The Real Aspect of the Gohonzon," WND-1, 832).

It is important that we revere Nam-myoho-renge-kyo—the fundamental Law and the life state of Buddhahood embodied in the Gohonzon—believing and accepting that it is inherent in our own lives. By doing so, we can tap the Mystic Law that resides within us and manifest our inherent Buddhahood.

The Record of the Orally Transmitted Teachings states: "Great joy [is what] one experiences when one understands for the first time that one's mind from the very beginning has been a Buddha. Nam-myoho-renge-kyo is the greatest of all joys" (OTT, 211–12).

When we realize that we are inherently Buddhas and Nam-myoho-renge-kyo itself, we can bring forth in our lives wonderful benefit and good fortune without measure. There is no greater joy in life.

When we triumph over hardships through our practice of the Mystic Law, we will lead lives of unsurpassed joy while developing a state of eternally indestructible happiness.

CHAPTER

3

Attaining Buddhahood in This Lifetime and Kosen-rufu

Attaining Buddhahood in This Lifetime

B**uddhahood is the** state of awakening that a Buddha has attained. The word *enlightenment* is often used synonymously with Buddhahood. Buddhahood is regarded as a state of perfect freedom, in which one is awakened to the eternal and ultimate truth that is the reality of all things. This supreme state of life is characterized by boundless wisdom, infinite compassion, and undaunted courage.

The fundamental purpose of our Buddhist faith and practice is to attain the life state of Buddhahood.

The purpose of practicing Nichiren Buddhism, in addition to attaining Buddhahood in this lifetime on an individual level, is to secure happiness for others as well.

By embracing faith in the Gohonzon and striving sincerely in Buddhist practice for oneself and others, anyone can realize the state of Buddhahood in this existence. This is the principle of attaining Buddhahood in this lifetime.

Practice for oneself means to carry out Buddhist practice for one's own benefit. Practice for others means to teach and guide others to

Buddhist practice so that they, too, can experience benefit. Specifically, practice for oneself and others indicates doing gongyo and chanting daimoku, Nam-myoho-renge-kyo, while also reaching out to talk with others about Buddhism, teaching and guiding them and thereby propagating the Mystic Law.

Nichiren Daishonin wrote:

> If votaries of the Lotus Sutra carry out religious practice as the sutra directs, then every one of them without exception will surely attain Buddhahood within his or her present lifetime. To cite an analogy, if one plants the fields in spring and summer, then, whether it be early or late, one is certain to reap a harvest within the year. ("The Doctrine of Three Thousand Realms in a Single Moment of Life," WND-2, 88)

Attaining Buddhahood, or becoming a Buddha, does not mean becoming some kind of special human being completely different from who we are now, nor does it mean being reborn in a pure land far removed from this world in our next lifetime.

The Daishonin explains the "attain" of attaining Buddhahood as follows: "'Attain' means to open or reveal" (OTT, 126). Attaining Buddhahood, therefore, simply means revealing our innate Buddhahood.

As ordinary people, we can reveal this enlightened state of life just as we are. This is expressed in the Buddhist concepts of "the attainment of Buddhahood by ordinary people" and "attaining Buddhahood in one's present form."

Attaining Buddhahood does not mean going to some other world. Rather, it means establishing a state of absolute and indestructible happiness here in the real world.

The Daishonin says that "one comes to realize and see that each thing—the cherry, the plum, the peach, the damson—in its own entity, without undergoing any change, possesses the eternally endowed three bodies [of a Buddha]"[1] (OTT, 200). As this passage suggests, attaining Buddhahood means living in a way in which we make the most of our unique inherent qualities and develop our potential to the fullest.

In other words, in attaining Buddhahood our lives are purified, allowing us to give full expression to their inherent workings; we gain a strong inner state that is not swayed by any hardship.

Attaining Buddhahood is not the achievement of a final goal. The state of Buddhahood is characterized by an unremitting struggle based on faith in the Mystic Law to eliminate evil and generate good. Those who strive tirelessly for kosen-rufu are Buddhas.

The Attainment of Buddhahood by Ordinary People and Attaining Buddhahood in One's Present Form

The terms *ordinary person* or *common mortal* appear frequently in Buddhist sutras and texts, indicating an unenlightened person. The Lotus Sutra teaches that ordinary people inherently possess the life state of Buddhahood and that they can reveal that state of life. That is, it is possible for us to manifest within us that noble life state as ordinary people. This is expressed in such Buddhist terms as "ordinary people are identical with the highest level of being" (OTT, 22) and "an ordinary person is a Buddha" ("The Izu Exile," WND-1, 36).

Attaining Buddhahood is a process of manifesting the life state of a Buddha, which is originally present within all people (the inherent world of Buddhahood). A Buddha, therefore, is not a special being separate from or superior to human beings. The Daishonin taught that attaining Buddhahood is revealing the highest humanity—that is, Buddhahood—in our lives as ordinary people.

This is called "attaining Buddhahood in one's present form." This means that people can realize the life state of a Buddha just as they are without having to be reborn and changing their present form as an ordinary person.

Though Mahayana sutras other than the Lotus Sutra teach the attainment of Buddhahood, they all require at least two conditions.

The first is that one not belong to any of the following groups, which were deemed incapable of attaining Buddhahood: practitioners of the two vehicles (voice-hearers and cause-awakened ones), evil people, and women.

Practitioners of the two vehicles believed that it was impossible for them to attain the elevated life state of the Buddha and so contented themselves with seeking to gain the stage of arhat—the highest stage of awakening in the teachings for the voice-hearers. These practitioners aimed for the annihilation of body and mind in arriving at this stage, in which all earthly desires were completely extinguished, ending the cycle of rebirth into this world. Many Mahayana sutras harshly condemned such practitioners as being unable to attain Buddhahood.

These sutras also taught that evil people had to first be reborn as good people and women be reborn as men before they could attain Buddhahood. Neither evil people nor women were considered able to attain Buddhahood as they were. Though these sutras taught the possibility of attaining Buddhahood, only a limited number of people could meet the requirements to actually do so.

The second condition for attaining Buddhahood in Mahayana sutras other than the Lotus Sutra was that one had to engage in Buddhist practice over repeated cycles of birth and death (known as countless kalpas of practice) in order to free oneself from the life state of an unenlightened, ordinary person and achieve the life state of a Buddha.

In contrast, the Lotus Sutra teaches that attaining Buddhahood is not a matter of becoming some sort of exceptional or extraordinary being but that each person can reveal the life state of Buddhahood within them just as they are.

Nichiren Daishonin further clarified that the fundamental Law by which all Buddhas attain enlightenment is Nam-myoho-renge-kyo. He also manifested his enlightened state of life that is one with that Law in the form of the Gohonzon—the object of devotion of Nam-myoho-renge-kyo.

By embracing faith in the Gohonzon of Nam-myoho-renge-kyo, anyone can reveal the Buddhahood inherent in his or her life.

Nichikan[2] wrote, "If we accept and believe in this object of devotion and chant Nam-myoho-renge-kyo to it, then our lives are themselves the object of devotion of three thousand realms in a single moment of life; we are the founder, Nichiren Daishonin."

By believing in the Gohonzon and continuing to exert ourselves in faith and practice for the sake of kosen-rufu, we can manifest in our lives as ordinary people the same life state of Buddhahood as Nichiren Daishonin.

This is also expressed as the principles of attaining Buddhahood in one's present form and attaining Buddhahood in this lifetime.

Earthly Desires Are Enlightenment and the Sufferings of Birth and Death Are Nirvana

The idea of attaining Buddhahood in one's present form can be expressed from another distinct perspective as the principles that earthly desires are enlightenment and the sufferings of birth and death are nirvana.

Even ordinary people whose lives are dominated by earthly desires, burdened by negative karma, and afflicted by suffering can, by awakening to the reality that Buddhahood exists within their own lives, manifest the wisdom of a Buddha's enlightenment, liberate themselves from suffering, and realize a state of complete freedom.

A life tormented by earthly desires and suffering can become a life of limitless freedom that shines with enlightened wisdom just as it is. This is the meaning of the principle that earthly desires are enlightenment.

Nichiren Daishonin teaches that the world of Buddhahood within us is Nam-myoho-renge-kyo.

When we believe in the Gohonzon, chant Nam-myoho-renge-kyo, and awaken to our true, noble selves, then the wisdom to live out our lives, the courage and confidence to face the challenges of adversity and overcome them, and the compassion to care for the welfare of others will well forth from within us.

The sufferings of birth and death are nirvana means that though we may be in a state of suffering caused by the painful realities of birth and death, when we believe in the Gohonzon and chant Nam-myoho-renge-kyo, we can manifest in our lives the tranquil life state of a Buddha's enlightenment (nirvana).

The principles of earthly desires are enlightenment and the sufferings of birth and death are nirvana teach us that when we base ourselves on faith in the Mystic Law, we can lead positive, proactive lives, transforming every problem and suffering we have into a cause for growth and happiness.

Relative Happiness and Absolute Happiness

Second Soka Gakkai president Josei Toda (1900–58) taught that there are two kinds of happiness: relative happiness and absolute happiness. Relative happiness describes a condition in which our material needs are fulfilled and our personal desires satisfied. But desires know no limits; even if we may enjoy a sense of those desires being fulfilled for a time, it is not lasting. Since this kind of happiness is dependent on external circumstances, if those circumstances should change or disappear, then so will our happiness. Such happiness is called relative because it exists only in relation to external factors.

In contrast, absolute happiness is a state of life in which being alive itself is a source of happiness and joy no matter where we are or what our circumstances. It describes a life condition in which happiness wells forth from within us. Because it is not influenced by external conditions, it is called absolute happiness. Attaining Buddhahood means establishing this state of absolute happiness.

Living amid the realities of this world, it is inevitable that we will meet with various problems and difficulties. But in the same way that someone who is strong and physically fit can easily climb a mountain, even when carrying a heavy load, those who have established an inner state of absolute happiness can use any challenge they encounter as an impetus for bringing forth powerful life force and calmly overcome adversity. For strong mountain climbers, the steeper and more demanding the ascent, the greater enjoyment they feel in overcoming each challenge on the path to the summit. Similarly, for those who through Buddhist practice have acquired the life force and wisdom to overcome hardships, the real world with all its troubles and challenges is a place for creating value rich in satisfaction and fulfillment.

In addition, while relative happiness, which depends on external factors, disappears with death, the absolute happiness of the life state of Buddhahood persists eternally. As the Daishonin says, "Passing through the round of births and deaths, one makes one's way on the land of the Dharma nature, or enlightenment, that is inherent within oneself" (OTT, 52).

Establishing the Correct Teaching for the Peace of the Land and Kosen-rufu

As guidelines for practice in order to secure happiness for oneself and others amid the realities of society, Nichiren Daishonin stressed the importance of establishing the correct teaching for the peace of the land and kosen-rufu.

Establishing the Correct Teaching for the Peace of the Land

Nichiren Buddhism is a teaching that enables people to transform their life condition and develop a state of absolute happiness in the course of this lifetime. In addition, through such a profound inner transformation in each individual, it aims to achieve peace for society as a whole.

The Daishonin sets forth the principle for realizing peace in his treatise "On Establishing the Correct Teaching for the Peace of the Land."

"Establishing the correct teaching" means promoting faith in and acceptance of the correct teaching of Buddhism as the foundation for people's lives and making the Buddhist teaching of respect for the dignity of life the fundamental motivating principle of society. "For the peace of the land" means realizing peace and prosperity in society as well as safety and security for all individuals in their daily lives.

In addition to indicating the nation as a political institution centering on the ruling authorities, "land" in "On Establishing the Correct Teaching for the Peace of the Land" refers, on a deeper level, to the basis of people's daily lives and sustenance. In that sense, it refers to not only the social structure formed by human beings but also the land itself—the natural environment.

The Daishonin's belief that the people are the central presence in the land may perhaps also be discerned in his frequent usage in the treatise's original manuscript of the Chinese character for "land" (also, "country" or "nation") written with the element for "people" inside a rectangular enclosure. He used this rather than the more commonly used element for "king," or that suggesting a military domain, inside a rectangular enclosure.

The Daishonin also wrote, "A king sees his people as his parents" ("Offerings in the Snow," WND-2, 809), asserting that those in power should make the people their foundation. He further warned that rulers who "fail to heed or understand the afflictions of the populace" will fall into the evil paths (see "On the Protection of the Nation," WND-2, 92).

While "On Establishing the Correct Teaching for the Peace of the Land" was written to realize peace in Japan at that time, its underlying spirit is to achieve peace and security for the people and, further, to actualize peace for the entire world and happiness for all humanity into the distant future.

The Daishonin wrote this treatise and remonstrated with the ruling authorities out of his wish to put an end to the sufferings of the people of his day. He was showing through his own example that practitioners of Buddhism must not content themselves with a Buddhist practice that consists solely of praying for their own enlightenment. Rather, basing themselves on the principles and spirit of Buddhism, they must actively engage in seeking solutions to the problems and issues facing society.

In "On Establishing the Correct Teaching for the Peace of the Land," the Daishonin wrote, "If you care anything about your personal security, you should first of all pray for order and tranquillity throughout the four quarters of the land, should you not?" (WND-1, 24).

The self-centered attitude exemplified by averting one's gaze from society's problems and withdrawing into a realm of religious faith alone is sternly repudiated in Mahayana Buddhism.

The Soka Gakkai today is engaged in efforts to resolve global issues through its activities in the areas of peace, culture, education, and human rights, based on the principles and ideals of Nichiren Buddhism. These efforts, too, directly accord with the principle and spirit of establishing the correct teaching for the peace of the land articulated by the Daishonin.

Kosen-rufu

The aim of Buddhism is to share and spread the correct teaching that embodies the Buddha's enlightenment and to guide all people toward attaining the life state of Buddhahood and actualizing peace and prosperity for all humanity.

For that reason, Shakyamuni Buddha states in the Lotus Sutra, "After I have passed into extinction, in the last five-hundred-year period you must spread it [this teaching] abroad widely throughout Jambudvipa [the entire world] and never allow it to be cut off, nor must you allow [negative forces such as] evil devils, the devils' people, heavenly beings, dragons, yakshas, kumbhanda demons, or others to seize the advantage!" (LSOC, 330).

This passage states that in the last five-hundred-year period—meaning this present period of the Latter Day of the Law—the Mystic Law should be spread abroad widely throughout the entire world. "Spread abroad widely" here is a translation of the Chinese characters pronounced kosen-rufu in Japanese.

In the Lotus Sutra, the Buddha also entrusts the mission of widespread propagation, or kosen-rufu, in the Latter Day of the Law to the Bodhisattvas of the Earth, who as his disciples from the unimaginably remote past are bodhisattvas who have thoroughly forged themselves.

During the preaching of the Lotus Sutra, countless multitudes of such bodhisattvas emerge from the earth. Led by Bodhisattva Superior Practices, they vow to propagate the Mystic Law, the essence of the Lotus Sutra, after Shakyamuni's passing.

Shakyamuni in turn predicts that after his death these Bodhisattvas of the Earth will appear in this suffering-filled world and like the sun and the moon illuminate the darkness of people's lives and lead them to enlightenment.

Kosen-rufu Is the Fundamental Spirit of Nichiren Daishonin

In exact accord with the aforementioned passage of the Lotus Sutra, Nichiren Daishonin strove to spread the great Law of Nam-myoho-renge-kyo in the evil age of the Latter Day while enduring numerous life-threatening persecutions.

The Daishonin touches upon the widespread propagation of the Mystic Law, or kosen-rufu, as follows:

> The "great vow" refers to the propagation of the Lotus Sutra [Nam-myoho-renge-kyo]. (OTT, 82)

> If Nichiren's compassion is truly great and encompassing, Nam-myoho-renge-kyo will spread for ten thousand years and more, for all eternity, for it has the beneficial power to open the blind eyes of every living being in the country of Japan, and it blocks off the road that leads to the hell of incessant suffering. ("On Repaying Debts of Gratitude," WND-1, 736)

> When I, Nichiren, first took faith in the Lotus Sutra, I was like a single drop of water or a single particle of dust in all the country of Japan. But later, when two people, three people, ten people, and eventually a hundred, a thousand, ten thousand, and a million people come to recite the Lotus Sutra [chant Nam-myoho-renge-kyo] and transmit it to others, then they will form a Mount Sumeru of perfect enlightenment, an ocean of great nirvana. Seek no other path by which to attain Buddhahood! ("The Selection of the Time," WND-1, 580)

From these passages we can clearly see that achieving kosen-rufu, the widespread propagation of the Mystic Law, is the fundamental spirit of the Nichiren Daishonin.

The Daishonin also repeatedly urged his followers to dedicate their lives to kosen-rufu, attain Buddhahood, and actualize the principle of establishing the correct teaching for the peace of the land.

The Soka Gakkai—Making Kosen-rufu a Reality

The Soka Gakkai is the harmonious gathering of Buddhist practitioners who have inherited and carry on the Daishonin's spirit, spreading the Mystic Law just as he taught in his writings.

The Daishonin wrote, "If you are of the same mind as Nichiren, you must be a Bodhisattva of the Earth" ("The True Aspect of All Phenomena," WND-1, 385). The Soka Gakkai, which has spread the Mystic Law in the same spirit as the Daishonin, is the organization of Bodhisattvas of the Earth fulfilling the mission of kosen-rufu.

Until the appearance of the Soka Gakkai seven hundred years after the Daishonin's death, no one had been able to widely spread the Mystic Law. It is the Soka Gakkai that has made the predictions of Shakyamuni and Nichiren Daishonin a reality. This is proof that the Soka Gakkai is the organization that has emerged to carry out the mission of kosen-rufu, acting in accord with the Buddha's intent.

The Soka Gakkai is making kosen-rufu a reality, spreading the Mystic Law throughout the entire world, just as the Lotus Sutra teaches.

NOTES:

1. The three bodies of a Buddha refer to the Dharma body, the fundamental truth, or Law, to which a Buddha is enlightened; the reward body, the wisdom to perceive the Law; and the manifested body, the compassionate actions a Buddha carries out to lead people to happiness.

2. Nichikan (1665–1726) was a scholar priest who lived during the Edo period (1603–1868) of Japan. He systematized and placed fresh emphasis on the Buddhist principles of Nichiren Daishonin as inherited and transmitted by his direct disciple and successor, Nikko Shonin.

CHAPTER

4

The Ten Worlds

This chapter will discuss the principle known as the Ten Worlds and clarify that the fundamental aim of faith in Nichiren Buddhism is to reveal in our lives the state of Buddhahood that is inherent within us.

The Six Paths

The Ten Worlds is a classification of ten distinct states of life and forms the foundation for the Buddhist view of life. Through examining the Ten Worlds, we can come to understand the nature of our own state of life and gain insights into how we can transform it.

The Ten Worlds are (1) the world of hell, (2) the world of hungry spirits [hunger], (3) the world of animals [animality], (4) the world of asuras, (5) the world of human beings [humanity], (6) the world of heavenly beings [heaven], (7) the world of voice-hearers [learning], (8) the world of cause-awakened ones [realization], (9) the world of bodhisattvas, and (10) the world of Buddhas.

The first six worlds—those of hell, hungry spirits, animals, asuras, human beings, and heavenly beings—are known as the six paths.

The remaining four—those of voice-hearers, cause-awakened ones, bodhisattvas, and Buddhas—are known as the four noble worlds.

According to the ancient Indian worldview, the six paths refer to the six realms of existence among which life transmigrates in the unending cycle of birth and death. Buddhism adopted this concept. The four noble worlds are life states that are attained through Buddhist practice.

In Buddhist sutras other than the Lotus Sutra, the Ten Worlds are regarded as ten separate, fixed realms of existence. The Lotus Sutra, however, fundamentally rejects that point of view, teaching that the Ten Worlds are ten states of life inherent within each living being. It reveals that living beings of the nine worlds from hell through bodhisattvas possess within them the world of Buddhas and that Buddhas also possess all the other nine worlds.

Therefore, a being presently manifesting one of the Ten Worlds in fact possesses within itself all of the Ten Worlds and can subsequently manifest any other of the Ten Worlds in response to external influences. This teaching that all of the Ten Worlds are inherent within one another is called the mutual possession of the Ten Worlds.

Nichiren Daishonin writes: "Neither the pure land nor hell exists outside oneself; both lie only within one's own heart. Awakened to this, one is called a Buddha; deluded about it, one is called an ordinary person" ("Hell Is the Land of Tranquil Light," WND-1, 456).

A single life possesses all the Ten Worlds. This means that even if right now we may be experiencing the painful life state of hell, we can transform it into the supremely joyous life state of Buddhahood. The principle of the Ten Worlds based on the Lotus Sutra opens the way for such dynamic inner transformation.

Let us now examine the nature of each of the Ten Worlds. First of all, with regard to the lowest six worlds, or the six paths, the Daishonin writes in "The Object of Devotion for Observing the Mind":

10 Worlds

Ten potential states or conditions a person can manifest or experience.

1 Hell

2 Hunger (hungry spirits)

3 Animality (animals)

4 *Asuras*

THE FOUR EVIL PATHS

5 Humanity (human beings)

6 Heaven (heavenly beings)

THE SIX PATHS

7 Learning (voice-hearers)

8 Realization (cause-awakened ones)

THE TWO VEHICLES

9 Bodhisattva

10 Buddhahood

THE FOUR NOBLE WORLDS

> When we look from time to time at a person's face, we find him or her sometimes joyful, sometimes enraged, and sometimes calm. At times greed appears in the person's face, at times foolishness, and at times perversity. Rage is the world of hell, greed is that of hungry spirits, foolishness is that of animals, perversity is that of asuras, joy is that of heaven, and calmness is that of human beings. (WND-1, 358)

Based on this passage, let us look at each of the six paths in turn.

The World of Hell

The Japanese word for hell, *jigoku* (Sanskrit *naraka*), literally means underground prison. Buddhist scriptures describe many hells, such as the eight hot hells, the eight cold hells, and numerous others.

The world of hell is the lowest state of life, a state in which one is imprisoned by suffering and completely lacking in freedom.

The Daishonin writes, "Hell is a dreadful dwelling of fire" ("Letter to Niike," WND-1, 1026). Hell is a life state in which we experience the world around us as a place that inflicts suffering upon us as intense as if we were being burned by flames.

In "The Object of Devotion for Observing the Mind," the Daishonin says, "Rage is the world of hell." This rage arises from bitter frustration and discontent with ourselves for not being or achieving what we desire or toward the world around us that inflicts such suffering on us. It is the tormented expression of a life hopelessly trapped in a realm of suffering.

Hell is the state of being in which living is itself extremely painful and everything we see is colored by our unhappiness and misery.

The World of Hunger

The world of hungry spirits, or the life state of hunger, is characterized by relentless craving and the suffering arising from such craving going unsatisfied.

In ancient Indian mythology, hungry spirits (Sanskrit *preta*) originally referred to the deceased or spirits of the dead, who were believed to be constantly starving. As a result, a life state where one is spiritually and physically tormented by intense, unremitting craving came to be known as the world of hungry spirits.

The Daishonin writes: "Greed is [the world] of hungry spirits" and "The realm of hungry spirits is a pitiful place where, driven by starvation, they devour their own children" ("Letter to Niike," WND-1, 1026). Hunger so strong that it drives those in its grip to devour their own children describes a life state of suffering in which one's heart and mind are ruled by insatiable desires.

Of course, wants and desires have both good and bad aspects. Human beings could not survive without the urge to eat. Desires can also be the motivating force for human progress and self-improvement. But the life state of hunger is one of suffering in which one is enslaved by desires and unable to use them for constructive, creative purposes.

The World of Animality

The world of animals, or the life state of animality, is characterized by foolishness in the sense of being moved by impulse rather than reason and being concerned only with immediate benefit and gratification.

The Daishonin writes, "Foolishness is [the world] of animals." This describes a life state of acting impulsively for short-term benefit with no understanding of the law of cause and effect and no ability to judge between right and wrong, good and evil.

The Daishonin also writes of the world of animals: "It is the nature of beasts to threaten the weak and fear the strong" ("Letter from Sado," WND-1, 302) and "[The realm of] animals is to kill or be killed" ("Letter to Niike," WND-1, 1026). He describes the life state of animality as one ruled by the law of the jungle, a struggle for survival in which one is willing to harm others to stay alive with no sense of reason or conscience. Because it is a condition of foolishness, in which one is fixated on immediate reward and cannot give thought to future consequences, those dominated by this life state are the engineers of their own suffering and self-destruction.

[Note: The use of the term *animals* is based on ancient Indian beliefs. Naturally, there are examples of animals, such as service dogs, that devotedly assist others, and it is also true that some of the behavior of human beings—for example, wars and genocide—is often much crueler and more brutal than that of nonhuman animals.]

Because the worlds of hell, hungry spirits, and animals all represent conditions of suffering, they are collectively known as the three evil paths.

The World of Asuras

Asuras are contentious demons found in ancient Indian mythology.

A characteristic of the world of asuras is an obsession with personal superiority or self-importance, a tendency to always compare oneself with others and want to be better than them.

When those in this life state encounter people they consider inferior to themselves, they become arrogant and look down on them. Even when they recognize that others are superior to them in some way, they are unable to respect them. And when they meet someone who is truly more powerful than they are, they become cowardly and fawning.

Those in the world of asuras often put on an appearance of being people of virtue and fine character, even pretending to be humble in order to impress others. Inside, however, they are filled with jealousy and resentment toward those they perceive to be better than them. This gap between outward appearance and inner reality leads to hypocrisy and self-deception, which are also characteristics of this life state.

This is why the Daishonin writes, "Perversity is [the world] of asuras" (WND-1, 358). Here, "perversity" means concealing one's true feelings in order to ingratiate oneself with others. There are two aspects to this perversity—to fawn and deceive and to distort reason.

Unlike those in the three evil paths—the worlds of hell, hungry spirits, and animals—who are dominated by the three poisons of greed, anger, and foolishness,[1] those in the world of asuras act of their own volition. In this sense, the world of asuras can be considered a higher state than the three evil paths. Nevertheless, because it is essentially a realm filled with suffering, it is grouped together with the three evil paths to form the four evil paths.

The World of Humanity

The world of human beings, or the life state of humanity, is a calm, composed state in which people maintain their characteristic human qualities. The Daishonin says, "Calmness is [the world] of human beings" (WND-1, 358).

Those in the life state of humanity understand the principle of cause and effect and are rational enough to know the difference between good and evil.

The Daishonin writes, "The wise may be called human, but the thoughtless are no more than animals" ("The Three Kinds of Treasure," WND-1, 852). Those in the life state of humanity have the capacity to distinguish right from wrong and to exercise self-control.

The life state of humanity cannot be sustained without effort. In the reality of society, which is filled with many negative influences, it is indeed difficult for people to live in a humane way. It is impossible without a constant effort at self-improvement and personal development. The world of humanity is the first step toward a life state of winning over oneself.

Those in the world of humanity are also seen as the correct vessel for attaining the noble paths.[2] While they are vulnerable to falling into the evil paths through negative influences, they also have the potential to advance to the four noble worlds, or enlightened states of life, through Buddhist practice.

The World of Heaven

In ancient Indian cosmology, heaven referred both to gods possessing supernatural powers and to the realm where they lived. In ancient India, it was believed that those who performed good acts in their present life would be reborn as deities in the heavenly realm.

In Buddhism, the world of heavenly beings, or the life state of heaven, is regarded as a condition of joy experienced when we fulfill our desires through effort. The Daishonin writes, "Joy is [the world] of heaven" (WND-1, 358).

There are all kinds of desires—instinctive desires such as for food and sleep, material desires for things like a new car or house, social desires such as the wish for status and honors, and intellectual and spiritual desires such as the aspiration to know about yet-to-be-discovered worlds or create new works of art. The state of blissful joy one experiences upon fulfilling these various kinds of desires is the world of heavenly beings.

But the joy of the world of heavenly beings is not lasting. It fades and disappears with the passage of time. In that sense, the world of heavenly beings is not the state of genuine happiness that should be our ultimate aim.

The Four Noble Worlds

The worlds from hell to heavenly beings discussed above, together referred to as the six paths, are easily influenced by external circumstances.

When one's desires are fulfilled, one experiences the bliss of the world of heavenly beings, and when one's external environment is calm and stable, one enjoys the tranquility of the world of human beings. But should those external conditions change, one can quickly tumble into states of intense suffering, such as the worlds of hell and hungry spirits.

In the sense that they are governed by external circumstances, the life states of the six paths are not truly free or autonomous.

The aim of Buddhist practice is to transcend the six paths and develop a self-determined state of happiness that is not controlled by external circumstances. The awakened states of life a person can develop through Buddhist practice are known as the four noble worlds—the worlds of voice-hearers, cause-awakened ones, bodhisattvas, and Buddhas.

The Worlds of Learning and Realization

Traditionally, the worlds of voice-hearers and cause-awakened ones were life states attained through practicing the so-called Hinayana teachings.

People in these two worlds, which are also known as the life states of learning and realization, are together referred to as the people of the two vehicles.

The world of voice-hearers is the life state attained by those who gain a partial awakening through hearing the Buddha's teaching.

The world of cause-awakened ones refers to the life state attained by those who gain a partial awakening through their own observations and effort. It is also called the realm of self-awakened ones.

The partial awakening of the people of the two vehicles is an awakening to the impermanence of all phenomena—the reality that all things are constantly changing, coming into and going out of existence. Those in the worlds of voice-hearers and cause-awakened ones, by objectively observing themselves and the world around them, perceive the truth that all things arise in response to causes and conditions, change with the passage of time, and eventually cease to exist. And they strive to overcome their attachment to transient things and phenomena.

There are times in our daily lives when we have a strong perception of the impermanence of all things, including ourselves. The Daishonin notes: "The fact that all things in this world are transient is perfectly clear to us. Is this not because the worlds of the two vehicles are present in the human world?" (WND-1, 358). He is saying that the world of human beings also possesses these perceptive worlds of voice-hearers and cause-awakened ones.

Those who sought to attain the life states of the two vehicles identified the cause of suffering as attachment to impermanent, transient things and phenomena, and they endeavored to eradicate such attachment and other earthly desires. Because of that, however, they strayed into the mistaken path of seeking to extinguish their own bodies and minds entirely (the teaching of reducing the body to ashes and annihilating consciousness).[3]

From the perspective of the enlightenment of the Buddha, the awakening gained by those in the worlds of learning and realization is imperfect and partial. But those in these worlds content themselves with this lesser degree of enlightenment and do not seek the full enlightenment of the Buddha. Though they acknowledge the superior enlightenment of the Buddha, their teacher, they do not think themselves able to attain it and remain at a lower level of enlightenment.

Additionally, those in the worlds of voice-hearers and cause-awakened ones are inclined to self-absorption, seeking only their own enlightenment and making no effort to help others do the same. This self-centeredness is the limitation of these two worlds.

The World of Bodhisattvas

The Sanskrit term *bodhisattva* means a living being (*sattva*) who strives continuously to attain the enlightenment (*bodhi*) of a Buddha. Although the people of the two vehicles accept the Buddha as their teacher, they do not believe themselves capable of attaining the same life state as the Buddha. In contrast, bodhisattvas not only regard the Buddha as their teacher, but they strive to obtain the same enlightened state. In addition, they also try to lead others to enlightenment by communicating and spreading the Buddha's teachings.

What distinguishes those of the world of bodhisattvas, or the life state of bodhisattva, is their seeking spirit to attain the highest life state of Buddhahood and their altruistic efforts to share the benefits they have obtained through Buddhist practice.

The bodhisattva spirit is to empathize with the pain and sorrow of others and work to relieve that suffering and impart joy out of a wish for the happiness of oneself and others.

Whereas the people of the two vehicles, focused solely on their own welfare, content themselves with a lesser awakening, those in the world of bodhisattvas act with a sense of mission for the sake of people and the Law.

The essence of the world of bodhisattvas is compassion. The Sanskrit term for compassion, *karuna* (Jpn *jihi*), is sometimes translated as "loving-kindness" or "mercy." In "The Object of Devotion for Observing the Mind," the Daishonin writes: "Even a heartless villain loves his wife and children. He too has a portion of the bodhisattva world within him" (WND-1, 358). Just as even the most heartless villain still cares for his own wife and children, a spirit of compassion for others is inherent in all life. Those in the life state of bodhisattva direct this spirit of compassion to all people and make it the foundation for their lives.

The World of Buddhahood

The world of Buddhas, or the life state of Buddhahood, is the supremely noble life state manifested by a Buddha.

Buddha means awakened one—one who has awakened to the Mystic Law, the fundamental Law that pervades the entire universe and all life. Specifically, it refers to Shakyamuni, who lived in India. The Buddhist sutras describe various other Buddhas such as Amida Buddha, but these are all fictitious beings symbolizing an aspect of the greatness of the enlightened life state of Buddhahood.

Nichiren Daishonin is the Buddha of the Latter Day of the Law who as an ordinary human being revealed the infinitely respectworthy life state of Buddhahood in his own life and established the path by which all people can attain enlightenment.

Buddhahood is an expansive life state overflowing with good fortune and benefit attained through awakening to the fact that the Mystic Law is the foundation of one's being. Having attained this state of life, a Buddha is able to manifest unsurpassed wisdom and compassion, employing them unceasingly to enable all people to attain the same life state of enlightenment that he enjoys.

The life state of Buddhahood is originally inherent in our own beings. It is difficult to manifest it, however, in our daily lives, which are filled with unending problems and challenges. For this reason, the Daishonin inscribed the Gohonzon, or object of devotion, as a means for all people to bring forth from within them the life state of Buddhahood. The Gohonzon embodies the enlightened life state of Nichiren Daishonin, the Buddha of the Latter Day of the Law, the essence of which is Nam-myoho-renge-kyo.

When we believe in the Gohonzon and chant Nam-myoho-renge-kyo for the happiness of ourselves and others, we can tap the life state of Buddhahood within us.

In the "The Object of Devotion for Observing the Mind," the Daishonin identifies the profound connection between the life state of Buddhahood and faith in the Mystic Law, saying, "That ordinary people born in the latter age can believe in the Lotus Sutra is due to the fact that the world of Buddhahood is present in the human world" (WND-1, 358).

The Lotus Sutra reveals that all people are inherently Buddhas; we human beings can believe in that teaching precisely because our lives fundamentally possess the state of Buddhahood.

Nichikan wrote, "Strong faith in the Lotus Sutra is called the world of Buddhahood."[4] "Lotus Sutra" here means the Gohonzon of Nam-myoho-renge-kyo—the Lotus Sutra of the Latter Day of the Law. Therefore, having strong faith to base our lives on the Gohonzon is nothing other than the life state of Buddhahood.

This life state of Buddhahood attained through faith in the Mystic Law can be described in contemporary terms as a state of absolute happiness that nothing can destroy. Second Soka Gakkai president Josei Toda described it as a state of life in which being alive is itself happiness.

The life state of Buddhahood is also often likened to the spirit of a lion king—a state of complete ease and confidence in which, like the lion king, one fears nothing.

NOTES:

1. Three poisons of greed, anger, and foolishness: the fundamental evils inherent in life that give rise to human suffering. In *The Treatise on the Great Perfection of Wisdom*, often attributed to the renowned Mahayana doctrinal master Nagarjuna, the three poisons are regarded as the source of all illusions and earthly desires. The three poisons are so called because they pollute people's lives and work to prevent them from turning their hearts and minds to goodness.

2. Correct vessel for attaining the noble paths: a passage found in *The Treatise on the Rise of the World* stating that human beings represent the most appropriate vessel, or form of life, for attaining the Buddha way.

3. Reducing the body to ashes and annihilating consciousness: a reference to the Hinayana doctrine asserting that one can attain nirvana, escaping from the sufferings of endless cycle of birth and death, only upon extinguishing one's body and mind, which are deemed to be the sources of earthly desires, illusions, and sufferings.

4. Translated from Japanese. Nichikan, "Sanju hiden sho" [The threefold secret teaching] in *Rokkansho* [The six-volume writings] (Tokyo: Seikyo Shimbun-sha, 1960).

CHAPTER

5

Three Proofs

The three proofs are three criteria for determining the correct teaching for leading people to absolute happiness. They demonstrate that the Buddhism of Nichiren Daishonin is the teaching that makes it possible for all people in the Latter Day of the Law to attain Buddhahood in this lifetime.

The three proofs are documentary proof, theoretical proof, and actual proof.

Documentary proof means that a religion's doctrines are based upon or in accord with its foundational scriptures.

Nichiren Daishonin writes, "One should accept what is clearly stated in the text of the sutras, but discard anything that cannot be supported by the text" ("Conversation between a Sage and an Unenlightened Man," WND-1, 109). Doctrines not supported by documentary proof amount to no more than arbitrary interpretations or opinions. In the case of Buddhism, all doctrines must be supported by the sutras, the teachings expounded by Shakyamuni. In the Soka Gakkai, the writings of Nichiren Daishonin, who practiced and embodied the essence of the Lotus Sutra, serve as documentary proof.

Theoretical proof, or proof of reason, means that a religion's doctrines and assertions are compatible with reason and logic. The Daishonin writes, "Buddhism is reason" ("The Hero of the World," WND-1, 839). Buddhism respects and values reason. One should not, therefore, accept irrational arguments or interpretations.

Actual proof means that belief and practice of a religion's doctrines produce positive results in one's life and daily affairs and in society.

Religion is not just an abstraction; it exerts a powerful influence on people's lives. We can judge the merits of a religion by examining this actual impact on people and society.

The Daishonin writes: "In judging the relative merit of Buddhist doctrines, I, Nichiren, believe that the best standards are those of reason and documentary proof. And even more valuable than reason and documentary proof is the proof of actual fact" ("Three Tripitaka Masters Pray for Rain," WND-1, 599). As is clear from this statement, the Daishonin valued actual proof above all other forms of proof. This is because the original aim of Buddhism is to help people become happy.

A religion is not truly credible if it lacks any of these three forms of proof—documentary proof; reason, or theoretical proof; and actual proof. To use an analogy, to be deemed safe and effective, any medicine must have a list of ingredients and their effects (documentary proof), be supported by a logical explanation for being effective (theoretical proof), and when taken, show real results in relieving the ailment it is intended to treat (actual proof).

Nichiren Buddhism has a basis that is objective and universally acceptable in terms of both theory and practical results.

CHAPTER

6

Faith, Practice, and Study

The purpose of Nichiren Buddhism is to enable us to transform our lives. There are three basic elements in applying its teachings: faith, practice, and study.

Faith means belief in the Buddhism of Nichiren Daishonin—the correct teaching of the Latter Day of the Law—and in the Gohonzon, its ultimate expression. The central ingredient of Buddhist practice is faith.

Practice refers to concrete efforts to transform and develop our lives.

Study means learning and inquiring into the teachings of Nichiren Buddhism. It provides us with guiding principles for proper faith and practice, helping us strengthen our practice and deepen our faith.

Correct practice of Nichiren Buddhism must include all three of these elements.

In "The True Aspect of All Phenomena," the Daishonin says:

> Believe in the Gohonzon, the supreme object of devotion in all of Jambudvipa [the entire world]. Be sure to strengthen your faith, and receive the protection of Shakyamuni, Many Treasures, and the Buddhas of the ten directions. Exert yourself in the two ways of practice and study. Without practice and study,

> there can be no Buddhism. You must not only persevere yourself; you must also teach others. Both practice and study arise from faith. Teach others to the best of your ability, even if it is only a single sentence or phrase. (WND-1, 386)

Faith

Faith is belief and acceptance—believing in and accepting a Buddha's teaching. Such faith is the foundation for attaining the life state of Buddhahood.

In the Lotus Sutra, it is taught that even Shariputra, who was known as foremost in wisdom among Shakyamuni's disciples, could grasp the essence of the sutra's teaching only through faith. In the "Simile and Parable," the third chapter of the Lotus Sutra, we find the passage "Even you, Shariputra, in the case of this sutra were able to gain entrance through faith alone" (LSOC, 109–10). This is the principle of gaining entrance through faith alone.

Only through faith can we attain the same great wisdom and life state as the Buddha. When we believe in and accept a Buddha's teaching, we can understand for the first time the correctness of the Buddhist philosophy of life.

Nichiren Daishonin, the Buddha of the Latter Day of the Law, inscribed Nam-myoho-renge-kyo, the fundamental Law of the universe to which he had awakened, in the form of the Gohonzon. In other words, in the Gohonzon, he revealed his enlightened life state of Buddhahood for the sake of all people in the Latter Day of the Law.

Therefore, the most important thing in practicing Nichiren Buddhism is having deep faith in the Gohonzon as the object of devotion for attaining the life state of Buddhahood. When we have faith in the Gohonzon and chant Nam-myoho-renge-kyo, we can tap the power of the Mystic Law in our lives and firmly establish the life state of Buddhahood within us.

Practice

Practice is the concrete actions we engage in based on faith in the Gohonzon.

Nichiren Buddhism teaches that Buddhahood, a life state of boundless wisdom and compassion, is inherent within our own lives.

The purpose of our Buddhist practice is to manifest our innate Buddhahood and attain a state of absolute happiness. To tap this latent potential and bring it to function in our lives, concrete efforts to transform and develop ourselves are essential. If we are to reveal our Buddhahood, we need to continue making efforts that accord with reason and correct Buddhist principles. This is what is referred to as practice.

Practice has two aspects—practice for ourselves and practice for others. These are compared to the two wheels of a cart: our practice must have both of these aspects to advance properly.

Practice for ourselves means striving to gain personal benefit from practicing Nichiren Buddhism. Practice for others is teaching others about Buddhism so that they may also receive benefit.

The Daishonin states: "Now, however, we have entered the Latter Day of the Law, and the daimoku that I, Nichiren, chant is different from that of earlier ages. This Nam-myoho-renge-kyo encompasses both practice for oneself and the teaching of others" ("On the Receiving of the Three Great Secret Laws," WND-2, 986).

In the Latter Day of the Law, both our practice for ourselves—seeking personal enlightenment—and our practice for others—sharing Buddhism with others so that they may also attain enlightenment—are based on practicing the fundamental teaching for attaining Buddhahood, Nam-myoho-renge-kyo.

Therefore, correct practice in Nichiren Buddhism encompasses both these forms of practice. It consists of chanting Nam-myoho-renge-kyo with faith in the Gohonzon while also teaching others about the benefit of faith in the Gohonzon and encouraging them to practice as well.

Specifically, practice for ourselves means doing gongyo (reciting excerpts of the Lotus Sutra and chanting Nam-myoho-renge-kyo), and practice for others means sharing and spreading the teachings of Buddhism. In addition, the various activities we carry out as Soka Gakkai members for the sake of kosen-rufu also constitute practice for others.

The Daily Practice of Gongyo and Efforts to Spread the Teachings

Gongyo refers to reciting portions of the Lotus Sutra and chanting Nam-myoho-renge-kyo before the Gohonzon. This is the first of the two aspects of the practice for transforming our lives.

Comparing the practice of gongyo to polishing a mirror, the Daishonin writes:

> This is similar to a tarnished mirror that will shine like a jewel when polished. A mind now clouded by the illusions of the innate darkness of life is like a tarnished mirror, but when polished, it is sure to become like a clear mirror, reflecting the essential nature of phenomena and the true aspect of reality. Arouse deep faith, and diligently polish your mirror day and night. How should you polish it? Only by chanting Nam-myoho-renge-kyo. ("On Attaining Buddhahood in This Lifetime," WND-1, 4)

As this metaphor indicates, the mirror itself doesn't change, but when it is polished, the way that it functions changes. Similarly, through our continuous daily practice of gongyo, we can polish and strengthen our lives and positively transform the way they function.

Referring to the importance of spreading the correct teaching of Buddhism, the Daishonin states in "The True Aspect of All Phenomena": "You must not only persevere yourself; you must also teach others. . . . Teach others to the best of your ability, even if it is only a single sentence or phrase" (WND-1, 386). And in "Letter to Jakunichi-bo" he says, "Those who become Nichiren's disciples and lay believers should realize the profound karmic relationship they share with him and spread the Lotus Sutra as he does" (WND-1, 994).

It is important that we seek not only to transform our own state of life through our daily practice of gongyo but to share the teachings of Buddhism with others, even if only a single word, aiming for the happiness of both ourselves and others.

Such efforts help deepen our own faith and practice as well as activate the altruistic life states of bodhisattva and Buddhahood within us—motivating us to work for the happiness and well-being of others. They enable us to become genuine disciples of Nichiren Daishonin. Along with doing gongyo, efforts to spread the teachings of Buddhism are also a powerful force for transforming our lives.

The Lotus Sutra states:

> If one of these good men or good women in the time after I have passed into extinction is able to secretly expound the Lotus Sutra to one person, even one phrase of it, then you should know that he or she is the envoy of the Thus Come One [the Buddha]. He has been dispatched by the Thus Come One and carries out the Thus Come One's work. (LSOC, 200–201)

Based on this passage, the Daishonin declares, "One who recites even one word or phrase of the Lotus Sutra and who speaks about it to another person is the emissary of Shakyamuni Buddha, lord of the teachings" ("The Pure and Far-Reaching Voice," WND-1, 331).

In other words, the efforts we make in our practice for others' happiness are truly noble: they constitute the behavior and practice of the Buddha, which we carry out as the Buddha's emissaries.

Primary Practice and Supporting Practice

Our morning and evening practice of gongyo is a central pillar of our efforts to transform our lives.

In gongyo, we chant Nam-myoho-renge-kyo with faith in the Gohonzon and recite portions of the Lotus Sutra—an extract from "Expedient Means," the second chapter, and the verse section of "Life Span," the sixteenth chapter.

Chanting Nam-myoho-renge-kyo with faith in the Gohonzon is fundamental; it is therefore called the "primary practice."

Reciting the "Expedient Means" and "Life Span" chapters helps bring forth the benefit of the primary practice; it is therefore called the supporting practice.

The reason we recite the "Expedient Means" and "Life Span" chapters is that these are the two most important chapters of the Lotus Sutra, which opens the way to enlightenment for all people. The "Expedient Means" chapter explains the true aspect of all phenomena, the central doctrine of the theoretical teaching, or first fourteen chapters, of the Lotus Sutra. The "Life Span" chapter reveals the Buddha's attainment of enlightenment in the remote past, the central doctrine of the essential teaching, or latter fourteen chapters, of the sutra. The Daishonin writes, "If you recite the 'Life Span' and 'Expedient Means' chapters, then the remaining chapters will naturally be included even though you do not recite them" ("The Recitation of the 'Expedient Means' and 'Life Span' Chapters," WND-1, 71).

Explaining the relationship between the primary practice and supporting practice, Nichikan,[1] compared them to food and seasoning, respectively. He compared it to how, when eating rice or noodles, the primary source of nourishment, seasonings such as salt or vinegar are used to enhance, or supplement, the flavor. In similar fashion, reciting the "Expedient Means" and "Life Span" chapters, he said, helps bring forth the profound benefit of the primary practice of chanting Nam-myoho-renge-kyo, which is why it is called the supporting practice.[2]

In reciting the "Expedient Means" and "Life Span" chapters, then, we praise and enhance the beneficial power of the Gohonzon.

Study

Study is the study of the Buddhist teachings, primarily reading the writings of Nichiren Daishonin and studying the correct principles and doctrines of Nichiren Buddhism. Through such study, we can develop a deeper, more solid faith and ensure that we practice correctly.

Without Buddhist study, we are at risk of lapsing into our own personal interpretations of Buddhism and may easily be deceived by those presenting erroneous teachings.

As the Daishonin affirms when he writes "Both practice and study arise from faith" ("The True Aspect of All Phenomena," WND-1, 386), faith is the foundation of study.

President Toda said, "Faith seeks understanding, and understanding deepens faith."[3] The purpose of studying and deepening our understanding of Buddhism, as he notes, is to deepen our faith.

The Daishonin urges his disciples to study his writings over and over. He writes, for instance, "Have him read this letter again and again, and listen attentively" (WND-1, 1031). In addition, he praises the seeking spirit of disciples who asked him questions about the Buddhist teachings.

Nikko Shonin, the Daishonin's direct disciple and successor, stated: "Followers of this school should engrave the writings of the Daishonin in their lives" (GZ, new ed., 2196; GZ, 1618)[4] and "Those of insufficient Buddhist learning who are bent on obtaining fame and fortune are not qualified to call themselves my followers" (GZ, new ed., 2196; GZ, 1618.)[5] In this way, he encourages us to study the Daishonin's writings.

NOTES:

1. Nichikan (1665–1726) was a scholar priest who lived during the Edo period (1603–1868) of Japan. He systematized and placed fresh emphasis on the Buddhist principles of Nichiren Daishonin as inherited and transmitted by his closest disciple and immediate successor, Nikko Shonin.

2. Paraphrased from Japanese. Nichikan, "Toryu gyoji sho" [The practice of this school] in *Rokkansho* [The six-volume writings] (Tokyo: Seikyo Shimbun-sha, 1960).

3. Translated from Japanese. Josei Toda, *Toda Josei zenshu* [The complete writings of Josei Toda], vol. 4 (Tokyo: Seikyo Shimbun-sha, 1989), 18.

4. Translated from Japanese. "Nikko yuikai okibumi" [The twenty-six admonitions of Nikko], article 11.

5. "Nikko yuikai okibumi," article 8.

CHAPTER

7

Faith for Overcoming Obstacles

Life is invariably accompanied by difficulties. And in our struggles for kosen-rufu, we are sure to encounter hardships and obstacles. In this section, we explore the various kinds of obstacles and hindrances that will arise in the process of carrying out our Buddhist practice and affirm the significance of faith for overcoming obstacles.

Because our aim is to attain Buddhahood in this lifetime, it is important that we maintain our Buddhist faith and practice throughout our lives. However, Buddhism teaches that as we continue to persevere in our practice, obstacles and difficulties will arise without fail to obstruct us. It is crucial, then, that we be prepared for these and strive to establish faith that cannot be compromised by any problem or adversity.

Why is it, then, that a person who upholds the correct teaching encounters obstacles?

First, it is because to believe in and practice the correct teaching with the aim of developing the life state of Buddhahood means transforming one's life at the deepest level. And while any change or reformation will be met with some resistance, Buddhist practice in particular arouses strong opposition to change from within our own lives or our relationships with others. This may be compared to the way the resistance of the water on the hull of a moving boat produces waves.

The hindrances that arise as we practice Buddhism for the purpose of attaining enlightenment are often categorized as the three obstacles and four devils. In addition to these, the Lotus Sutra teaches that a votary of the Lotus Sutra, a person who correctly practices and endeavors to spread its teaching in the evil and impure age of the Latter Day of the Law, will encounter opposition by forces known as the three powerful enemies.

These represent the persecutions that occur wherever there are those who, in the evil age after the passing of Shakyamuni Buddha, actively practice the Lotus Sutra and work to spread it widely with the wish of enabling all people to attain Buddhahood. Persecution by the three powerful enemies can be proof that one is a genuine votary or practitioner of the Lotus Sutra.

The Three Obstacles and Four Devils

In his work "Letter to the Brothers," Nichiren Daishonin writes:

> One passage from the same volume [the fifth volume of T'ien-t'ai's *Great Concentration and Insight*] reads: "As practice progresses and understanding grows, the three obstacles and four devils emerge in confusing form, vying with one another to interfere. . . . One should be neither influenced nor frightened by them. If one falls under their influence, one will be led into the paths of evil. If one is frightened by them, one will be prevented from practicing the correct teaching." This statement not only applies to me, but also is a guide for my followers. Reverently make this teaching your own, and transmit it as an axiom of faith for future generations. (WND-1, 501)

As this passage teaches, when we believe in and practice the correct Buddhist teaching and advance in our Buddhist practice while deepening our faith, functions will arise to obstruct our progress. These are known as the three obstacles and four devils.

In the same work, the Daishonin explains the elements of the three obstacles and four devils in some detail as follows:

> The three obstacles in this passage are the obstacle of earthly desires, the obstacle of karma, and the obstacle of retribution. The obstacle of earthly desires is the impediments to one's practice that arise from greed, anger, foolishness, and the like; the obstacle of karma is the hindrances presented by one's wife or children; and the obstacle of retribution is the hindrances caused by one's sovereign or parents. Of the four devils, the workings of the devil king of the sixth heaven are of this last kind. (WND-1, 501)

The Three Obstacles

First, in the "three obstacles," the word *obstacles* indicates functions that hinder us in our faith and practice. These are categorized as the obstacle of earthly desires, the obstacle of karma, and the obstacle of retribution.

The obstacle of earthly desires indicates when earthly desires, or impulses and afflictions such as greed, anger, and foolishness (called the three poisons), prevent us from progressing in Buddhist faith and practice.

The obstacle of karma refers to hindrances to our faith and practice that result from our evil acts in this life. In this passage from "Letter to the Brothers," opposition from those close to one, such as one's spouse or children, is cited as a specific example.

The obstacle of retribution describes impediments to our Buddhist practice that are due to the difficult circumstances into which we are born or have come to live. These are considered adverse rewards or reckoning that stem from bad karma formed in past lifetimes. In "Letter to the Brothers," the Daishonin associates these with opposition coming from people whose wishes one is bound to follow, such as the sovereign of one's nation and one's parents.

The Four Devils

Next, the word *devil* of the "four devils" refers to workings that deprive those who believe in and practice Buddhism of the brilliance in their lives that is an embodiment of the Mystic Law. The four devils are (1) the hindrance of the five components,[1] (2) the hindrance of earthly desires, (3) the hindrance of death, and (4) the hindrance of the devil king.

The hindrance of the five components arises from disharmony among the workings of the body and mind (the five components) of those who carry out faith and practice.

The hindrance of earthly desires means the emergence within one's life of afflictions such as greed, anger, and foolishness that function to destroy one's faith.

The hindrance of death comes when a person's Buddhist practice is cut short due to his or her death. Also, it can be said that one has been defeated by the hindrance or devil of death when the death of another practitioner, or of anyone close, causes one to doubt one's Buddhist faith.

Finally, there is the hindrance of the devil king. Devil king is an abbreviation of the Devil King of the Heaven of Freely Enjoying Things Conjured by Others—the king who makes free use of the fruits of others' efforts for his own pleasure. Also known as the devil king of the sixth heaven, this is the most fundamental kind of devilish function described in Buddhism.

Nichiren Daishonin says that "the fundamental darkness manifests itself as the devil king of the sixth heaven" ("The Treatment of Illness," WND-1, 1113). He means that this devilish function is something that emerges from the fundamental delusion innate in life itself. It reveals itself in different forms and utilizes various means to persecute and oppress those who are practicing Buddhism correctly. Most typically, it appears in the lives of those in power or who have strong influence over practitioners.

"The Wise Will Rejoice While the Foolish Will Retreat"

It is clear, then, that as we endeavor to carry out our Buddhist practice, obstacles and hardships will emerge to hinder our progress. However, it is important to be aware that earthly desires such as greed, anger, and foolishness, spouses and partners, children, parents, our own body and mind, or even death do not in themselves constitute obstacles and devils. Rather, what causes them to function as the three obstacles and four devils is the weakness of our own life force that allows us to be influenced negatively by them.

Even Shakyamuni was able to attain enlightenment through clearly recognizing that the various illusions arising within his own mind were devilish functions trying to prevent him from achieving his goal. For us, the key to defeating devilish functions is to develop faith that is strong enough to remain unshaken by anything.

In this regard, Nichiren Daishonin states:

> There is definitely something extraordinary in the ebb and flow of the tide, the rising and setting of the moon, and the way in which summer, autumn, winter, and spring give way to each other. Something uncommon also occurs when an ordinary person attains Buddhahood. At such a time, the three obstacles and four devils will invariably appear, and the wise will rejoice while the foolish will retreat. ("The Three Obstacles and Four Devils," WND-1, 637)

When the three obstacles and four devils appear, it is crucial to have the conviction that this is the very time for us to make great progress toward attaining Buddhahood and, as wise people who rejoice at such challenges, to persevere in our faith and overcome them.

The Three Powerful Enemies

"Encouraging Devotion," the thirteenth chapter of the Lotus Sutra, describes in a twenty-line verse section[2] the three kinds of powerful opponents who will persecute those who strive to spread the sutra's teachings in the Latter Day of the Law. Known as the three powerful enemies, they are defined as arrogant lay people, arrogant monks, and arrogant false sages.

All are described as arrogant because they display various kinds of haughtiness and conceit, believing themselves superior to or greater than other people.

1. Arrogant laypeople are those ignorant of Buddhism who persecute practitioners of the Lotus Sutra. The sutra explains that they will subject the sutra's practitioners to slander, cursing and speaking ill of them, or even attacking them with weapons such as swords and staves.

2. Arrogant monks are Buddhist clergy who slander the Lotus Sutra's practitioners. Because their understanding is flawed and their hearts crooked, they fail to understand the truth of the Buddhist teachings. And yet, attached to their own ways of thinking and believing themselves superior to others, they harass and persecute those who uphold the correct teaching.

3. Arrogant false sages are seemingly respectworthy monks or priests whom people regard as sages. Typically, they reside in

> places removed from society. Consumed with greed and the desire for profit, they harbor ill will and contrive to undermine or deceive practitioners of the Lotus Sutra. Their usual tactic is to approach the ruler, senior officials, or others in authority and make false claims about the practitioners, such as declaring them to be persons of mistaken views, in an attempt to motivate those in power to oppress them.

The Lotus Sutra describes the condition in which a person's heart or mind falls under the influence of such evil with the statement "Evil demons will take possession of others" (LSOC, 233). It teaches that in the Latter Day of the Law, those who practice the sutra will be repeatedly assailed and driven off by those who have succumbed to evil impulses.

Of these three powerful enemies, it is said that though one may be able to endure the first and the second, the third is the most formidable and pernicious. The reason is that it is quite difficult to perceive and recognize the true nature of such esteemed religious figures of high status—arrogant false sages.

In the Latter Day of the Law, whenever there are those who spread the teachings of the Lotus Sutra, these three powerful enemies will appear and attempt to interfere and obstruct such efforts. Because of his efforts to spread the Lotus Sutra, Nichiren Daishonin faced persecutions brought about by these three powerful enemies just as the sutra predicts, thus proving that he was the votary of the Lotus Sutra in the Latter Day.

NOTES:

1. The five components: The constituent elements of form, perception, conception, volition, and consciousness that unite temporarily to form an individual living being.

2. In Kumarajiva's Chinese translation of the Lotus Sutra, the three powerful enemies are described in twenty lines of the "Encouraging Devotion" chapter's verse section.

CHAPTER

8

Changing One's Karma

Nichiren Buddhism is a teaching that enables people to transform their lives at the deepest level, break through the limitations of karma, or destiny, and open a way forward. It is a teaching for changing one's karma for the better and securing a truly happy state of life today that will endure long into the future. In this section, we will examine the concept of changing one's karma, as well as the value of regarding our karma as our mission in this life.

Changing One's Karma

Life involves all kinds of problems and suffering, some of which are clearly the results of actions and choices we have made in this lifetime. But we also face problems for which we cannot identify the cause. At such times we may think: "I haven't done anything wrong. Why should I have to suffer like this?"

From the perspective of Buddhism, we can regard this latter kind of suffering as a result in this present life of negative actions we have taken in past existences. This is explained as the principle of karma.

The term *karma* originates from a Sanskrit word meaning

action. Our actions in past lifetimes that have the power to influence whether we are happy or unhappy in this life constitute our karma from past lifetimes, or destiny. Though this karma may be either good or bad, most often it refers to bad karma—the accumulation of negative causes from past lives resulting in suffering in the present.

Buddhism expounds the three existences of life and cause and effect spanning the three existences. That is, it views life as not limited to the present existence but as a continuum extending from past lives to the present and on to future lives. Actions made in past existences form causes, which appear as effects, or results, in the present existence; and actions taken in the present create causes that will bring about effects in future existences.

If one has created bad causes in a past life, then one will experience the results of those causes in this life as suffering; whereas if one has formed good causes in past lives, these will bring about pleasant effects in this life, such as good fortune, peace, and happiness. This is the general description of causality found in Buddhism, which underlies the concept of karma.

According to this view, however, even if we should become aware of the causes of our present suffering, we could do little to resolve it in this lifetime. As long as the causes from past lifetimes remain, we will experience suffering. Moreover, these causes will be cleared up only after they produce effects. In that case, all we can do is wait for one bad cause and then another to produce its effect until all bad causes are exhausted, while taking care not to produce any more bad causes. But this would take innumerable lifetimes. As such, this perspective on karma inspires little hope for improving our lives, and worse, it may lead us to simply resign ourselves to our fate.

Nichiren Daishonin shows us how to change our karma, or destiny, in this lifetime. In his "Letter from Sado," the Daishonin states that the great persecutions he has been facing cannot be attributed to the general explanation of cause and effect found in Buddhism but rather to the fact that he has in the past slandered the Lotus Sutra and its practitioners. He writes:

> My sufferings, however, are not ascribable to this causal law. In the past I despised the votaries of the Lotus Sutra. I also ridiculed the sutra itself, sometimes with exaggerated praise and other times with contempt. (WND-1, 305)

In the above passage, the Daishonin suggests that slandering or disparaging the Lotus Sutra—that is, committing slander of the correct teaching—is the most fundamental negative cause a person can make. The Lotus Sutra embodies the ultimate Buddhist principles that all people can attain Buddhahood, that all people should be respected, and that one must strive to achieve happiness both for oneself and for others. For that reason, slandering the Lotus Sutra means disparaging or denying the true potential and dignity of human beings and represents the ultimate form of evil, giving rise to all kinds of bad causes.

The Daishonin tells us that we can achieve a truly happy state of life in this world if we stop committing the ultimate evil of disbelieving and slandering the correct teaching and instead carry out the ultimate good of believing, protecting, and spreading it. That is, by replacing the most evil cause with the greatest good cause, the corresponding result will also be transformed into good. Core to this transformation is chanting Nam-myoho-renge-kyo.

The Daishonin quotes the Universal Worthy Sutra,[1] considered the epilogue to the Lotus Sutra, where it states, "The host of sins, like frost or dew, can be wiped out by the sun of wisdom" (LSOC, 390), saying:

> The "host of sins" are karmic impediments . . . and these are like frost or dew. Thus, although they exist, they can be wiped out by the sun of wisdom. The "sun of wisdom" is Nam-myoho-renge-kyo. (OTT, 205)

By believing in the Gohonzon and striving to chant Nam-myoho-renge-kyo for our own and others' happiness, we bring the sun of Buddhahood to rise within our lives, causing the negative karma from our many past lifetimes to vanish like frost or dew in the sunlight.

Lessening One's Karmic Retribution

Though we are striving in our Buddhist practice, we will never be completely free of life's hardships. Obstacles and hindrances will arise as well in the course of our struggles for kosen-rufu. Nichiren Daishonin teaches that encountering such hardships and being able thereby to change our karma is actually a benefit of Buddhist practice called lessening one's karmic retribution.

The concept of lessening one's karmic retribution is explained as follows. Heavy karma accruing from serious offenses in previous lifetimes will bring about major suffering, not only in the present life but in future lifetimes as well. The beneficial power of our Buddhist practice, however—of believing in and striving to spread the correct teaching—enables us to receive the effects of such offenses in this single lifetime and in a much-diminished form. Not only that, we can also extinguish all of our negative karma from the unperceivable past.

Concerning this principle of lessening one's karmic retribution, the Daishonin states, "The sufferings of hell will vanish instantly" ("Lessening One's Karmic Retribution," WND-1, 199). The moment our evil karma is eliminated, we become free from the worst kind of suffering in this and future existences.

Hardships become important opportunities to rid ourselves of past negative karma and to forge our lives. In this regard, the Daishonin writes:

> Iron, when heated in the flames and pounded, becomes a fine sword. Worthies and sages are tested by abuse. My present exile is not because of any secular crime. It is solely so that I may expiate in this lifetime my past grave offenses and be freed in the next from the three evil paths [the realms of hell, hungry spirts, and animals]. ("Letter from Sado," WND-1, 303)

Voluntarily Assuming the Appropriate Karma

Those who persevere in faith even in the face of hardships, and through doing so transform their karma, will experience a great change in the meaning they derive from living.

In this regard, the Lotus Sutra explains the principle of voluntarily assuming the appropriate karma [to fulfill one's vow]. Living beings are born in particular times and places because of two different kinds of causes—that is, they are born either according to their wishes and vows or as a result of their karma.

In general, Buddhism explains that bodhisattvas are born into this world out of a wish to fulfill their vow, while ordinary people are born into their present circumstances as a result of their past karma.

On the other hand, the Lotus Sutra teaches that bodhisattvas who have accumulated great good fortune through their Buddhist practice in past lives voluntarily relinquish the rewards due them for their pure deeds and choose instead to be born into this impure world that is filled with evil. They do so because they feel compassion for living beings and wish to save them from suffering. As a result, these bodhisattvas, just like those ordinary people who are born into this evil world due to their bad karma, also experience suffering.

Taking this view, we can find new meaning in adversity. As people who overcome problems through faith, we can regard living in this evil world and enduring suffering not simply as a result of our bad karma but as an opportunity to fulfill our vow as bodhisattvas to lead people to happiness. While sharing people's suffering as our own, we can serve as models for others of how to overcome such suffering.

Regarding those who base their way of living on this principle of voluntarily assuming the appropriate karma [to fulfill one's vow], Ikeda Sensei has observed:

> We all have our own karma or destiny. But when we look it square in the face and grasp its true significance, then any hardship can help us lead richer and more profound lives. And our actions in battling our destiny set an example for and inspire countless others.
>
> In other words, when we change our karma into mission, we transform our destiny from playing a negative role to a positive one. Anyone who changes their karma into their mission is a person who has voluntarily assumed the appropriate karma. Therefore, those who keep advancing, while regarding everything as part of their mission, proceed toward the goal of transforming their destiny.[2]

NOTES:

1. The full title is the Sutra on How to Practice Meditation on Bodhisattva Universal Worthy.

2. Translated from Japanese. Daisaku Ikeda, *Gosho no sekai* [The world of Nichiren Daishonin's writings], vol. 2 (Tokyo: Seikyo Shimbun-sha, 2004), 324–25.

CHAPTER

9

Faith Equals Daily Life

Nichiren Buddhism is a religion that enables people to build an indestructible state of happiness amid the realities of living. To that end, it is very important to engage fully in the challenges and responsibilities of daily life while persevering in Buddhist faith and practice. Faith is the process of developing and improving one's life at the deepest level.

In this sense, Nichiren Buddhism is a religion that teaches us that true victory for human beings is to develop our humanity to the fullest. For that reason, it is important that we embody in our behavior the wisdom and life force we cultivate through our Buddhist practice, thereby winning the trust of others. In this section, we will delve into concepts that are core to the practice of Nichiren Buddhism. These include the causality of benefit and loss; heavenly gods and benevolent deities; the unity of many in body, one in mind; faith equals daily life; and the importance of one's behavior as a human being.

The Causality of Benefit and Loss

If we correctly believe in and uphold Nam-myoho-renge-kyo, the ultimate Law of life and the universe, then we will consistently enjoy the limitless benefit inherent in that Law. And the ultimate benefit we derive from the Mystic Law is the attainment of Buddhahood; that is, the establishment of an imperturbable state of happiness. Once we believe in and begin to practice the Mystic Law, we have embarked on a course that leads to the life condition of absolute happiness called Buddhahood. By basing our lives on the Mystic Law, we naturally come to live correctly and to develop such genuine happiness.

Regarding the element *ku* in the word *kudoku*, or benefit, Nichiren Daishonin says it "refers to the merit achieved by wiping out evil, while the element *toku* or *doku* refers to the virtue one acquires by bringing about good" (OTT, 148). When we strive in our Buddhist practice, we can wipe away negative or evil functions that shroud our inner life, such as deluded desires and impulses, suffering, and apprehension, and bring forth good and positive qualities, such as wisdom, serenity, and joy.

Just prior to this it states:

> The word "benefits" (*kudoku*) means the reward that is represented by the purification of the six sense organs. In general we may say that now Nichiren and his followers, who chant Nam-myoho-renge-kyo, are carrying out the purification of the six sense organs. (OTT, 147–48)

Purification of the six sense organs means purification of the eyes, ears, nose, tongue, body, and mind—that is, every aspect of one's life—so they may fully perform the positive functions they inherently possess. As a result, one will remain unshaken and unswayed when confronting any kind of difficulty and will unlock and reveal from within the powerful state of Buddhahood. Our Buddhist practice enables us to tap and manifest our Buddha nature, and clear proof of this will appear as benefit in our everyday affairs and over the course of our lives. We will be able to live each day filled with happiness and good fortune without fail.

In this regard, the Daishonin states:

> Believe in this mandala [Gohonzon] with all your heart. Nam-myoho-renge-kyo is like the roar of a lion. What sickness can therefore be an obstacle?
>
> It is written that those who embrace the daimoku of the Lotus Sutra [Nam-myoho-renge-kyo] will be protected by Mother of Demon Children and by the ten demon daughters. Such persons will enjoy the happiness of Wisdom King Craving-Filled and the good fortune of Heavenly King Vaishravana. Wherever your daughter may frolic or play, no harm will come to her; she will move about without fear like the lion king. (WND-1, 412)

This means that through the power of chanting Nam-myoho-renge-kyo, we will also be protected by the heavenly gods and benevolent deities, overcome the various problems and difficulties we face in life, and enjoy happiness and fortune. Wherever we are, we will possess a state of life comparable to a lion king that knows no fear.

And as the Daishonin's words "Those who now believe in the Lotus Sutra will gather fortune from ten thousand miles away" ("New Year's Gosho," WND-1, 1137) tell us, a person who practices the Mystic Law will derive good fortune and happiness from any situation or circumstance.

He further stated, "Fortune comes from one's heart and makes one worthy of respect" and "The believers in the Lotus Sutra . . . are like the sandalwood with its fragrance" (WND-1, 1137).

This last passage tells us that just as the sandalwood tree emits its special fragrance, those who uphold and practice the Mystic

Law will exude from within the fragrance of happiness and virtue, will be loved and trusted by others, and will be protected and supported in their daily endeavors and throughout their lives.

In contrast, those who slander or disparage the correct teaching of Buddhism and go against the principles of cause and effect will engrave bad causes in the depths of their beings. At the same time, they will experience actual loss in the context of their daily lives.[1] It might be said that such loss is actual proof of error that can serve as a warning one is falling into a course or pattern that will lead to unhappiness. By becoming aware of one's errors, reflecting on them, and seeking to correct one's attitude in faith or way of living, one can summon the resolve to practice the Mystic Law more deeply and sincerely.

Seen from a different perspective, the fact that those who act counter to the Mystic Law experience loss is one of the wonderful qualities of that Law in that it can function to lead them to the correct path and allow them to reclaim the benefit of their Buddhist practice. In this way, Nichiren Buddhism offers a clear explanation of the benefit accruing to those who believe in and uphold the Mystic Law and the loss experienced by those who disparage the Law.

Heavenly Gods and Benevolent Deities

Heavenly gods and benevolent deities refers to the various workings or functions that serve to protect a person who practices the correct Buddhist teaching. Forces that serve in this way are personified in Buddhist literature as gods or deities that protect and support those who uphold and practice the teaching and guard the land in which they live.

Heavenly gods are beings who inhabit the realm of heaven, and benevolent deities refers to those which support and protect human beings. Buddhism employed the image of gods to make it readily acceptable to the people in lands where it spread, but they can be thought of as representing protective functions in the environment.

The Heavenly Gods Protect Those With Strong Faith

If we practice the correct Buddhist teaching and do good to others, then our environment and the people around us will begin to work to protect and support us—that is, they will function as heavenly gods and benevolent deities on our behalf. Buddhist scriptures describe the correct teaching as the source of power for such gods and deities, calling it the flavor, or nourishment, of the Law.

The Daishonin states, "The protection of the gods depends on the strength of one's faith" ("General Stone Tiger," WND-1, 953). The strength of the protection we receive depends on the strength of our faith and practice as we uphold and protect the Mystic Law.

Many in Body, One in Mind

Many in body, one in mind is a most essential principle and guideline for forming unity based on faith for the purpose of advancing kosen-rufu. Many in body (also, different in body) means that our appearance, nature, qualities and talents, social position, and circumstances differ from one another. One in mind means that we share the same intention and purpose.

The fundamental goal of our Buddhist practice, and the great wish of the Buddha, is kosen-rufu—broadly teaching and spreading the Mystic Law to realize peace and happiness for all people. Mind of "one in mind" indicates faith, and one in mind means to join our hearts and minds in sharing the great wish and vow to achieve kosen-rufu.

In other words, while each of us gives free and full play to our individuality and distinctive qualities, displaying our unique potential to the highest degree, we aim together for the lofty goal of kosen-rufu. This is the meaning of many in body, one in mind.

In contrast, though everyone might be compelled to look and act the same, if each person possesses a different intent or goal, then a state of disorder will ensue. Such a condition is called one in body, different in mind.

In this regard, the Daishonin says:

> If the spirit of many in body but one in mind prevails among the people, they will achieve all their goals, whereas if one in body but different in mind, they can achieve nothing remarkable. . . . In contrast, although Nichiren and his followers are few, because they are different in body, but united in mind, they will definitely accomplish their great mission of widely propagating the Lotus Sutra. ("Many in Body, One in Mind," WND-1, 618)

If we advance while challenging and overcoming various problems and hardships through unity in faith, the Daishonin assures us, then Buddhism will spread without fail.

Ikeda Sensei has said:

> In modern terms, many in body, one in mind means an organization. Many in body means that each person is different—that people differ in their appearances, standing in society, circumstances, and individual missions. But as for their hearts—their hearts should be one; each person should be one in mind, united in faith.
>
> On the other hand, if one has a situation of many in body, many in mind, there will be no unity of purpose. In addition, the concept of one in body, one in mind means that people are coerced into uniformity, made to think, look, and act alike. This is akin to fascism, where people have no freedom; it ultimately leads only to a condition of one in body, many in mind, where people give the appearance of being united and committed to

> the same goal on the surface but in reality don't go along with that goal in their hearts. . . .
>
> Many in body means to allow each individual to give full play to his or her unique potential and individuality. One in mind means that everyone works together based on faith, sharing the same goal and purpose. This is true unity.[2]

With the unity of many in body, one in mind as our guide and standard, each of us can fully display our unique power and ability as we advance together in realizing the Daishonin's will for the accomplishment of kosen-rufu.

Faith Equals Daily Life

While religion holds a special place in people's spiritual lives, it is often seen as having little to do with the challenges of living or with real-world concerns. In Nichiren Buddhism, however, faith and daily life are not regarded as separate. The Daishonin wrote, "Regard your service to your lord as the practice of the Lotus Sutra" ("Reply to a Believer," WND-1, 905). "Service to your lord" in this passage would be comparable in today's terms to any responsibility or obligation we might have in business, at work, or in society in general.

This passage teaches that daily life is the venue for Buddhist practice. It is the context in which we demonstrate how we live as individuals with faith as our basis. Our regular conduct is none other than an expression of the workings of our inner life. And faith is the power that enables us to transform and fulfill our lives at the deepest level.

We face many issues and problems in the course of living, but when we continue making earnest efforts to deal with them based on chanting daimoku with faith in the Gohonzon, those very real struggles become the impetus for us to bring forth our innate

Buddha nature. In this way, our mundane challenges become the stage upon which we enact the drama of transforming our life at its essence.

In addition, when we make the vital energy and rich life state we cultivate through our Buddhist practice the basis for conducting our affairs and fulfilling our responsibilities, then our life circumstances will also naturally change for the better.

If we compare our faith to the roots of a tree, our daily lives can be compared to the tree's trunk and its branches that bear flowers and fruit. On the other hand, a life that lacks a foundation of faith will be like a rootless plant, easily carried away by whatever is happening in our environment. Nichiren Buddhism teaches that the deeper our roots of faith, the more stable and secure our personal life.

In this way, Nichiren Buddhism views faith and the way we live as one and inseparable. For that reason, the guidance of the Soka Gakkai includes the principle that faith equals daily life, which explains that one's daily life is an expression of one's Buddhist faith. It teaches that a practitioner of Nichiren Buddhism should strive to be trusted by people in society and to win in all aspects of living.

One's Behavior as a Human Being

Buddhism is a religion that teaches how to develop one's humanity to the fullest. For human beings, this is the meaning of true victory.

As the Daishonin states, "The purpose of the appearance in this world of Shakyamuni Buddha, the lord of teachings, lies in his behavior as a human being" ("The Three Kinds of Treasure," WND-1, 852).

Shakyamuni appeared in this world and expounded the Buddhist teachings. His purpose in doing so (the purpose of his advent) was nothing mysterious or special. It was simply to show people the best way to live as human beings.

In other words, we show proof of the power of our faith by consistently acting with good sense amid human society and by being people of fine character who are trusted and respected at work, in our communities, and by all those around us.

The noblest kind of human behavior is that which demonstrates respect for people. Specifically, these are actions that recognize the Buddha nature innate in the lives of all people, deeply cherish that Buddha nature, and show respect for everyone. Fundamental to this is living with a wish and vow to enable all people to manifest that nature, that is, attain Buddhahood. This is expressed in our actions to cherish and care for the person right in front of us.

The Lotus Sutra describes the practice of Bodhisattva Never Disparaging, which consists of respecting the potential for Buddhahood inherent in all people and for that reason venerating every person he meets. Even those unaware of the realm of Buddhahood within their own lives are still endowed with the Buddha nature and are capable of tapping that potential and bringing it forth. It is the spirit of Buddhism, therefore, to cherish all people as children of the Buddha, regarding each person's life with the highest respect and viewing all people as equal.

If that spirit prevails, then no violence or action will emerge that tramples on the well-being of others. Striving to bring about social change through dialogue grounded in the principle of respect for all people is the essence of Nichiren Buddhism.

In this evil age of the Latter Day of the Law, people's confusion grows stronger. The kind of thinking that leads to abuse and discrimination against others or to turning people into tools to serve one's selfish aims has become prevalent. There is no other way to transform society's tendency toward corruption and raise people's state of life than to spread the practice that embodies behavior that respects others, cherishes life, and upholds human dignity.

In addition, in order to improve society we must strongly challenge the kind of thinking that holds people in contempt and encourages their misconceptions. For that reason, behavior that spreads goodness and admonishes evil constitutes the core practice of Buddhism and produces clear proof of victory in life for us as Buddhists and as human beings.

NOTES:

1. Buddhism expounds the principle of cause and effect. One receives either positive or negative results depending on whether one's actions have been good or bad. In Buddhism there is no transcendental being, such as a god or gods, who bestows rewards or inflicts retribution. One incurs retribution, or negative results, as the natural outcome of one's offenses.

2. Translated from Japanese. Daisaku Ikeda, *Seishun taiwa* [Discussions on youth], vol. 1 (Tokyo: Seikyo Shimbunsha, 2006), 364.

CHAPTER

10

The History of the Soka Gakkai

In this chapter, we will examine the history of the Soka Gakkai by learning about the accomplishments of its three founding presidents, who dedicated their lives to kosen-rufu, and the spirit of the oneness of mentor and disciple they shared.

The Lotus Sutra is the scripture that makes clear Shakyamuni Buddha's intent, the real purpose of his teachings. The intent of the Buddha is that all people bring forth the wisdom of Buddhahood that has always been inherent within them and establish unshakable happiness for themselves and for others, creating the basis for peace throughout the world.

The Lotus Sutra describes those who strive to actualize this intent of the Buddha as bodhisattvas of the true Mahayana teaching. They do so by struggling against all kinds of obstacles to achieve a profound transformation in their own lives and the lives of others. Such bodhisattvas, the sutra teaches, appear in the age called the Latter Day of the Law after the passing of Shakyamuni Buddha. They work to spread the Lotus Sutra throughout the entire world and thereby realize the Buddha's purpose, a process we call kosen-rufu, the widespread propagation of the sutra's teaching. The bodhisattvas who shoulder this mission are called the Bodhisattvas of the Earth.

The leader of the Bodhisattvas of the Earth who appear in the Lotus Sutra is named Bodhisattva Superior Practices. Nichiren Daishonin awakened to his mission to fulfill the role of Superior Practices in the Latter Day, taking as his own the great desire and vow for kosen-rufu described in the sutra—the Buddha's will and mandate. He stood up to actualize that will and established the fundamental teaching and practice for freeing all people and all of society from suffering throughout the Latter Day. For this reason, the Daishonin is often referred to as the Buddha of the Latter Day of the Law.

Today, it is the Soka Gakkai that has inherited and is carrying on the Daishonin's spirit, deeply resolved to accomplish its mission of worldwide kosen-rufu and earnestly persevering in its efforts to actualize that goal. The leaders who have firmly established the practice, awareness, and resolve for achieving kosen-rufu in modern times are the Soka Gakkai's first three presidents: its first president, Tsunesaburo Makiguchi (1871–1944), its second president, Josei Toda (1900–1958), and third president, Daisaku (1928–2023). Together they are respected as the Soka Gakkai's three founding presidents.

These three founding presidents are often referred to using the honorific title Sensei, which is sometimes used alone and sometimes follows the family name.

Founding Soka Gakkai President Tsunesaburo Makiguchi

We can find the origins of the Soka Gakkai in the relationship of mentor and disciple that existed between the first president, Tsunesaburo Makiguchi, and the second president, Josei Toda. Both were educators.

Tsunesaburo Makiguchi was born on June 6, 1871, in the village of Arahama in today's Kashiwazaki City, Niigata Prefecture (on the Japan Sea coast). While in his early teens, he moved to Hokkaido, the northernmost of Japan's four main islands, where he lived under the care of a relative. There he exerted himself in his studies while working and eventually entered the Hokkaido Normal School (present-day Hokkaido University of Education). Upon graduating, he became a schoolteacher, and in 1901 he moved to Tokyo with the manuscripts for his first work, *Jinsei chirigaku* (The geography of human life), which was published in 1903. He later held the post of principal at several elementary schools in Tokyo.

Josei Toda was born on February 11, 1900, in a village called Shioya in present-day Kaga City, Ishikawa Prefecture (also on the Japan Sea coast). Around 1902, his family moved to the village of Atsuta in today's Atsuta Ward in Ishikari City, Hokkaido. After graduating from an ordinary and higher elementary school (roughly equivalent to finishing today's junior high school) in 1914, he studied on his own while working. Eventually, he received his teaching certificate and began his career as a teacher in the Hokkaido town of Yubari.

Mentor and Disciple Meet

From that time on, Toda was seeking a mentor in life, and upon visiting Tokyo, he met Makiguchi, who was by then the principal of an elementary school. The two readily took to each other. The former was forty-eight years old at the time, and the latter, nineteen. Before long, Toda began to teach at the school, regarding Makiguchi as his mentor in life and supporting him in every possible way.

[Note: After moving to Tokyo, Toda, while working, studied at the night school of Kaisei Middle School and attended night classes at Chuo University.]

The Establishment of the Soka Kyoiku Gakkai

As an educator engaged first hand in primary school education,

Makiguchi's hope and vow was to enable every child to succeed in creating personal happiness as a self-sufficient member of society. He applied himself to developing an approach to education that would make this possible.

He delved deeply into research and formulated a theory of value that could serve as a foundation for the unique pedagogy he would later systematize. In the process, he encountered the Buddhism of Nichiren Daishonin that clarified the principles and fundamental practice for enabling the kind of life transformation that would give rise to value creation in human society. In 1928, he took faith in Nichiren Buddhism as a member of Nichiren Shoshu—a Buddhist school that derived its teachings from the lineage of Nikko Shonin, the Daishonin's closest disciple and immediate successor. He was fifty-seven at the time.

Makiguchi recounts his state of mind after taking faith in Nichiren Buddhism, writing, "With an indescribable joy, I completely changed the way I had lived for almost sixty years."[1] As this statement suggests, he took the Daishonin's teaching as a principle for living and devoted himself to it. He regarded it as a source of power and energy for creating value and achieving actual positive results in the midst of society and in daily life.

Regarding his motivation for taking faith, Makiguchi recalls, "Encountering the Lotus Sutra, I realized the teachings of the sutra in no way contradict the principles of philosophy and science that form the basis of our daily lives."[2]

That same year, Toda followed his mentor in taking faith in Nichiren Buddhism.

On November 18, 1930, Makiguchi published the first volume of his *Soka kyoikugaku taikei* (The system of value-creating education). This work systemized his views and ideas on education and was intended as the first of twelve volumes (of which four were eventually published).

His disciple, Toda, personally helped fund the publishing project and collaborated in every aspect of its production, including organizing and editing Makiguchi's notes into a manuscript and dividing the content into chapters.

The publisher's imprint listed Tsunesaburo Makiguchi as the author, Josei Toda as the publisher and printer, and the Soka Kyoiku Gakkai (Value-Creating Education Society) as the publishing house. This was the first time the name Soka Kyoiku Gakkai had appeared in public, and for this reason the date of the work's publication, November 18, is celebrated as the date of the Soka Gakkai's founding.

[Note: After the society was virtually destroyed by the militarist government, as will be explained later, Toda restored and renamed it the Soka Gakkai.]

Soka means creation of value. The purpose of education and the purpose of life are the pursuit of happiness, and the name Soka expresses Makiguchi's thinking that the creation of value is integral to building happiness.

The conception of the word *soka* itself came about in the course of a discussion between the two innovative educators. We could say that the birth of the Soka Gakkai, then, was itself a crystallization of the united spirit of mentor and disciple.

Buddhist Practice Directly Connected to Nichiren Daishonin

In this way, the Soka Kyoiku Gakkai was born out of the bond of mentor and disciple. Gradually, its organizational structure became more defined and it began to grow.

While originally an association of educators interested in the principles of value-creating education, noneducators eventually began to join as well, and the Soka Kyoiku Gakkai became a group for the practice of Nichiren Buddhism, the power source for value creation.

Though a society of lay practitioners of the Nichiren Shoshu school of Buddhism, the Soka Kyoiku Gakkai conducted its affairs in a completely different manner than previously established Nichiren Shoshu lay societies. These groups of lay believers were each affiliated with a specific local temple and operated under the guidance of the chief priest of that temple. The Soka Kyoiku Gakkai, however, operated independently, under the leadership of President Makiguchi and General Director Toda. It did not rely on priests for its management or operation or for providing guidance pertaining to faith.

Nor was the form of Buddhist practice it encouraged constrained to visiting temples or participating in ceremonies such as funeral and memorial services, as was the case with most Buddhist schools in Japan, including Nichiren Shoshu. Rather, it taught a practice that was open to everyone, which aimed to enable each person to actualize happiness in the midst of life's real challenges and to contribute to the peace and prosperity of society.

Through holding discussion meetings and its leaders traveling to various regions to offer guidance and encouragement in faith, the Soka Kyoiku Gakkai grew steadily, reaching a membership of around three thousand.

Challenging Japan's Militarism

The militarist government, in its reckless rush to expand its war footing with State Shinto[3] as its spiritual pillar, endeavored to coerce uniformity of thought among Japan's populace. It placed Soka Kyoiku Gakkai discussion meetings and other activities under surveillance by the Special Higher Police, which was responsible for investigating so-called thought crimes.

At the time, the government was pressuring citizens to visit and offer prayers at Shinto shrines and to enshrine and worship talismans to the Sun Goddess, the mythical progenitor of the imperial lineage. In June 1943, the priests of Nichiren Shoshu, in fear of government repression, delivered to the Soka Kyoiku Gakkai the following request: "Why don't you accept the Shinto talisman?" This was made to Makiguchi in the presence of the high priest.

The posture of Nichiren Shoshu in accepting the government's demand to enshrine the talisman to the Sun Goddess constituted complicity in slander of the Law (slander of the correct Buddhist teaching). It was a violation of the teachings of Nichiren Daishonin and his successor, Nikko Shonin, from whom Nichiren Shoshu claimed lineage. Makiguchi adamantly refused to accept the Shinto talisman, and the Soka Kyoiku Gakkai thus persisted in upholding the Daishonin's teaching and example of strictly admonishing slander of the Law.

On July 6, Makiguchi, while visiting Shimoda in Izu, Shizuoka Prefecture, and Toda, in Tokyo, were taken into custody by detectives of the Special Higher Police. Ultimately, twenty-one leaders of the Soka Kyoiku Gakkai were arrested on suspicion of committing lèse-majesté (the crime of violating the dignity of the emperor) and violating the Peace Preservation Law.[4]

All those arrested were subjected to coercive interrogation, and most of them abandoned their faith. In the end, only Makiguchi and his trusted disciple Toda resisted, persisting in their faith. Makiguchi even explained the teachings of Nichiren Buddhism to the prosecutors and judges who questioned him. Both refused to buckle under the pressure of authority and persevered in upholding the right and just principles of Buddhism.

On November 18, 1944, at the age of seventy-three, Makiguchi passed away at the Tokyo Detention Center due to malnutrition and the weakness of age. Coincidentally, the day of his death was the anniversary of the Soka Gakkai's founding.

Throughout his life, he had lived and practiced as the Daishonin taught in his writings, never hesitant to risk his life to do so. He lived as a noble pioneer who revived in modern times the Daishonin's spirit of propagating the Mystic Law to lead the people from suffering to happiness.

Toda's Awakening in Prison

While in prison, Toda, in addition to exerting himself in chanting daimoku, from early 1944 began to read the Lotus Sutra and ponder it deeply. In the process, he experienced an awakening—a realization that the Buddha is life itself.

As he continued to chant and engage in profound contemplation, Toda also became aware that he himself was a Bodhisattva of the Earth who had been present at the Ceremony in the Air described in the Lotus Sutra and who was entrusted with the widespread propagation of the sutra's teaching in the age after Shakyamuni Buddha. Thus, in November 1944, he awakened to the deep conviction that "I, Toda, am a Bodhisattva of the Earth," whose mission it was to accomplish kosen-rufu.

Through the profound awakening he experienced in prison, he developed an immovable conviction in Nichiren Daishonin's teachings and resolved that it was his personal mission to ensure their propagation worldwide. The awakening that Toda experienced while in prison became the primary inspiration behind the revival of Buddhism in the modern age and the powerful progress of the Soka Gakkai as a religious group dedicated to the accomplishment of kosen-rufu.

At a memorial service for Makiguchi after the war, Toda addressed his departed mentor:

> In your vast and boundless compassion, you let me accompany you even to prison. As a result, I could read with my entire being the passage from the Lotus Sutra "Those persons who had heard the Law dwelled here and there in various Buddha lands, con-

> stantly reborn in company with their teachers" (LSOC, 178). The benefit of this was coming to know my former existence as a Bodhisattva of the Earth and to absorb with my very life even a small degree of the sutra's meaning. Could there be any greater happiness than this?[5]

This passage from "The Parable of the Phantom City," the seventh chapter of the Lotus Sutra, teaches that the bond between mentor and disciple is such that they will always be born together in a Buddha land, in a place where they will strive together to save people from suffering.

While most of those persecuted by the authorities discarded their faith, Toda's words express his sincere appreciation and resolve to repay his debt of gratitude to his mentor under any circumstances. In them, we catch a glimpse of the strength of this bond of mentor and disciple.

Second Soka Gakkai President Josei Toda

On July 3, 1945, Josei Toda emerged from prison, having endured two years of life in confinement, and stood up alone to carry on the will of his mentor, Tsunesaburo Makiguchi, for the accomplishment of kosen-rufu. As general director of the Soka Gakkai, he began immediately to undertake the reconstruction of the organization, which was in a state of ruin.

The people of Japan at the time were in the pit of despair, reeling from the destruction brought on by the war and the turmoil of its aftermath. State Shinto, which had been forced upon the populace, was now being repudiated, along with other beliefs and values espoused by the militarist government. Yet no new source of hope was to be found.

Toda was convinced that Nichiren Buddhism alone constituted

a spiritual principle powerful enough to lead the people away from suffering and confusion, and he stood up with a great wish and vow to spread its teachings widely. The organization's goal would be not only to carry out educational reform but also to accomplish kosen-rufu, that is, peace throughout the world and happiness for all people. In line with that purpose, he amended its name from Soka Kyoiku Gakkai (Value-Creating Education Society) to Soka Gakkai (Value Creating Society) and began again to hold discussion meetings and travel to outlying regions to offer guidance in faith.

Encounter Between Mentor and Disciple—Toda and Ikeda Meet

In 1947, Toda met the young Daisaku Ikeda, who would later become the third president of the Soka Gakkai.

Ikeda was born in the district of Omori, in Tokyo's Ota Ward, on January 2, 1928.

He grew up at a time when Japan was plunging into war: He was nine years old at the start of the Second Sino-Japanese War (1937)[6] and thirteen at the outbreak of the war with the United States in the Pacific theater of World War II (1941). As the war intensified, his four older brothers, all in the prime of their lives, were drafted into the military and sent into battle. To help support his family, Ikeda worked at a munitions factory. Suffering from tuberculosis, however, he spent his early youth in physical distress, thinking deeply about the questions of life and death.

When his eldest brother, Kiichi, had returned home temporarily from the battlefield, he described how much misery the war was causing the people of Asia. In addition, his family had been forced from their home, which burned in the air raids. Through these accounts and experiences, he had become bitterly aware of war's injustice and tragic cruelty.

After the war, the family learned that the eldest brother, who had been sent back to the battlefront, had been killed in combat in Burma (present-day Myanmar). Witnessing his mother's deep sadness on learning of her son's death, young Ikeda's sense that war was evil, a crime against humanity, strengthened and deepened. Searching for clear answers to the question of how to live, he delved into works of literature and philosophy.

It was in the midst of this quest that on August 14, 1947, he attended his first Soka Gakkai discussion meeting. There he encountered the man who would become his lifelong mentor, Josei Toda.

At the meeting that evening, Toda was delivering a lecture on Nichiren Daishonin's writing "On Establishing the Correct Teaching for the Peace of the Land." When Toda had finished lecturing, Ikeda asked him a series of questions, including "What is the correct way to live?"; "What is a true patriot?"; "What is the meaning of Nam-myoho-renge-kyo?"; and "What do you think about the emperor?"

Toda's answers were clear and well reasoned and infused with the deep conviction he had gained through his struggles against Japan's militarist government and during two years of unjust imprisonment. As he listened, the youth was struck with the sense that he could trust everything this man had said.

Ten days later, on August 24, Ikeda began his practice of Nichiren Buddhism. At the time, he was nineteen years old, and Toda, forty-seven.

In April the following year, Ikeda enrolled in night classes at Taisei Gakuin (present-day Tokyo Fuji University). In September, he began to attend Toda's lecture series on the Lotus Sutra. Taking Toda as his mentor, he deepened his study and understanding of Buddhism and vowed to live his life for the sake of kosen-rufu.

And in January 1949, he started to work at Toda's publishing company as the editor of a magazine for boys.

The Shared Struggle of Mentor and Disciple to Rebuild the Soka Gakkai

In July 1949, the Soka Gakkai launched publication of its monthly magazine, the *Daibyakurenge*. The inaugural issue carried an essay Toda had written, titled "The Philosophy of Life." Later, Toda's businesses, which had been struggling amid the effects of Japan's chaotic postwar economy, faced dire financial setbacks, and on August 24, 1950, he announced his intention to step down from his position as Soka Gakkai general director.

On that occasion, young Ikeda asked him, "Who will be my mentor from here on?" to which Toda replied, "Though I've caused you nothing but trouble, I am your mentor," affirming the unbreakable bond of mentor and disciple.

The disciple exerted himself fully to settle Toda's business affairs, solving the financial crisis. He resolved deeply in his heart to make it possible for Toda Sensei to take full leadership as president of the Soka Gakkai.

Ikeda had stopped attending night school so that he could fully support this mentor. In response Toda told him that he would personally instruct him and provide him with a broad education surpassing any he could obtain from a university. This private instruction, known as Toda University, continued for nearly a decade, until the year before Toda's death.

Amid this intensive struggle, Toda discussed with his most trusted disciple his vision for the future. This included the establishment of the organization's newspaper *Seikyo Shimbun* to wage a battle of the written word for the sake of kosen-rufu and the founding of Soka University. Both of these institutions came into being as a result of such dialogues between mentor and disciple.

Inauguration of the Second President

Having overcome his business troubles, Toda agreed, in response to requests from many members, to take on the position of Soka Gakkai president. His inauguration as the organization's second president took place on May 3, 1951, and on that occasion, he declared his vow to achieve a membership of 750,000 households.[7] There were only about three thousand members at the time, and no one believed it was possible to achieve the goal Toda had stated.

Before his inauguration as president, Toda implemented a restructuring of the Soka Gakkai. He instituted a chapter-based system as a foundation for future development and refreshed the organization's preparedness to take on the challenge of kosen-rufu.

Before his becoming president, the *Seikyo Shimbun* commenced publication on April 20. Its inaugural issue carried the first installment of Toda's serialized novel *Human Revolution*, which he authored under the pen name Myo Goku.[8]

"Human revolution" refers to the process by which, through the practice of Nichiren Buddhism, each individual achieves a transformation of their state of life, eventually leading to a transformation in the destiny of all humankind. Upholding the principle of human revolution based on his philosophy of life, Toda endeavored to spread Nichiren Buddhism as a teaching accessible and applicable to all people today.

Also, immediately after his inauguration, President Toda established in succession the women's division, the young men's division, and the young women's division.

At the same time, in the beginning of 1952 on Toda's instruction, Ikeda became chapter adviser to the Soka Gakkai's Kamata Chapter in Tokyo and led an effort that resulted in 201 new households joining in February. This represented a breakthrough, far surpassing the monthly membership increases achieved by any chapter until then, and became known as the historic February Campaign. It marked a turning point after which the Soka Gakkai's progress toward achieving its membership goal of 750,000 households accelerated rapidly.

Toda had been planning to publish a collection of Nichiren Daishonin's writings. He knew this would be indispensable to the correct study and understanding of the Daishonin's teachings and, therefore, progress toward kosen-rufu, the widespread propagation of Nichiren Buddhism.

He asked the accomplished Nichiren scholar Nichiko Hori to take charge of the compilation and editing. In April 1952, marking the seven hundredth observation of the Daishonin's establishment of his teaching, *Nichiren Daishonin Gosho zenshu* (The complete works of Nichiren Daishonin) was published. From that time on, every Soka Gakkai member used this book to earnestly study Nichiren Daishonin's teachings, and the spirit to base one's actions on the Daishonin's writings was established throughout the entire Soka Gakkai.

Battle Against the Devilish Tendencies of Power

In April 1955, the Soka Gakkai ran its first candidates in local assembly elections. It took this step based on the spirit of establishing the correct teaching for the peace of the land, which the Daishonin espoused in the course of his struggle for the people's happiness and a peaceful society.

In 1956, Ikeda inspired a remarkable increase in propagation throughout the Kansai region of western Japan, with Osaka Chapter achieving an unprecedented membership increase of 11,111 households in May. In the House of Councillors election held in July that year, a candidate running in the Osaka electoral district, whose campaign Ikeda had led, was elected, defying all predictions to the contrary.

It was an outcome so astonishing that a major daily newspaper in Japan reported it under the headline "What Was Thought Impossible Has Been Achieved!"

Three candidates endorsed by the Soka Gakkai had been elected to the House of Councillors, and from then on the organization became a focus of attention as a group with growing social influence. At the same time, vested powers and interests began to attempt unjustly to impede the organization.

In response to these attacks, Ikeda fought resolutely to protect the Soka Gakkai members. In June 1957, when the Yubari Coal Miners Union in the city of Yubari, Hokkaido, acted unjustly to suppress Soka Gakkai members' religious freedom, he went there immediately to address the issue. Declaring that the Soka Gakkai would adamantly oppose these abuses, he strove diligently to achieve a solution. This became known as the Yubari Coal Miners Union Incident.

On July 3, immediately after leaving Yubari, Ikeda was unjustly arrested by the Osaka Prefectural Police in what became known as the Osaka Incident. In April that year (1957), the Soka Gakkai had run a candidate in a by-election to fill a vacant House of Councillors seat in the Osaka electoral district, and some members involved in the campaign had been charged with violating election laws. Ikeda, as the person responsible for the election campaign, was baselessly accused of orchestrating the illegal activities.

July 3 is the same date on which, in 1945, Toda was released from prison. Years later, Ikeda referred to this in a haiku, writing, "On this day of release and of imprisonment [July 3] are found the bonds of mentor and disciple."

For fifteen days, Ikeda was subjected to harsh interrogation, during which the prosecutor threatened, "If you don't confess your guilt, we will arrest President Toda." Toda's health had by that time become very frail, and going to jail would have surely led to his death.

To protect his mentor's life, Ikeda confessed to the charges for the time being, resolved to prove his own innocence later in court. On July 17, he was released from the Osaka Detention Center.

For the next four and a half years, he waged an ongoing court battle, and finally on January 25, 1962, he was pronounced not guilty on all charges. The prosecutor affirmed the court's decision, declining the option to appeal.

Entrusting Kosen-rufu to Successors

On September 8, 1957, Toda delivered his Declaration for the Abolition of Nuclear Weapons,[9] which would become the start and keynote of the Soka Gakkai's peace movement. In it, based on the Buddhist principle of the sanctity and dignity of life, he identified nuclear weapons as a devilish creation that threatens to usurp humanity's inviolable right to live, calling use of such weapons an act of absolute evil.

In December 1957, the Soka Gakkai reached its membership goal of 750,000 households, which Toda had vowed to achieve. And in March the following year, it completed and donated the edifice called the Grand Lecture Hall at the Nichiren Shoshu head temple, Taiseki-ji. There, on March 16, six thousand youth from around Japan, led by Ikeda, gathered for a ceremony in which Toda entrusted them with every aspect of kosen-rufu. On that occasion, President Toda declared, "The Soka Gakkai is the king of the religious world!"

This day, March 16, on which these young successors were entrusted with the great wish and vow for kosen-rufu, came to be called Kosen-rufu Day in the Soka Gakkai.

On April 2, 1958, Toda passed away, having completed all he had set out to accomplish. He was fifty-eight. Basing himself on the awakening he achieved while in prison, he had rebuilt the Soka Gakkai and constructed an immovable foundation for the future of kosen-rufu.

Third Soka Gakkai President Daisaku Ikeda

After Josei Toda's death, Daisaku Ikeda, in the newly established position of general administrator (since June 1958), took full responsibility for the management and leadership of the Soka Gakkai, and on May 3, 1960, was inaugurated as the organization's third president.

In his speech on that occasion, he said, "Though I am young, from this day I will take leadership as a representative of President Toda's disciples and advance with you another step toward the substantive realization of kosen-rufu."[10] With this, his first "lion's roar" as president—made on the same date that Toda had been inaugurated as president in 1951—a new period of great development for the Soka Gakkai began.

On October 2 that year, Ikeda Sensei left Japan for North and South America, the first step in a journey to spread the teachings of Nichiren Buddhism around the world. In January 1961, he visited Hong Kong, India, and other destinations in Asia, and that October he traveled to Europe, initiating a surge of progress toward worldwide kosen-rufu.

In this way, Sensei opened a substantive path toward achieving the westward transmission of Buddhism and the spread of the Mystic Law throughout the entire world, which Nichiren Daishonin had predicted.

In 1965, under the pen name Ho Goku,[11] he began writing the novel *The Human Revolution*, which would be serialized in the *Seikyo Shimbun* newspaper and would eventually extend to twelve volumes. His purpose in doing so was to correctly transmit the history and spirit of the Soka Gakkai to future generations.

In the preface to the novel, he conveys its main theme, "A great human revolution in just a single individual will help achieve a change in the destiny of a nation and, further, will enable a change in the destiny of all humankind."[12] *The Human Revolution* portrays the efforts and struggles of the three founding presidents of the Soka Gakkai as they strove to build a foundation for the happiness and peace of humankind.

Sensei continued to chronicle the Soka Gakkai's history in *The New Human Revolution*, a thirty-volume novel also serialized in the *Seikyo Shimbun*.

A Movement for Peace, Culture, and Education

The Soka Gakkai is an organization that fosters youth who will contribute positively to society.

Toda said that when kosen-rufu advances, numerous capable individuals will emerge, playing important roles in various fields of society. He further expected that the Soka Gakkai would one day become an important mainstay for the flourishing of peace and culture for all humankind. To that end, he insisted that it must become an outstanding educational movement, one that can raise people capable of fulfilling their missions.

To actualize that vision, the Soka Gakkai under the leadership of Sensei has promoted a growing movement for peace, culture, and education grounded in Buddhist principles, thereby making great contributions to society.

In response to his proposals, the Soka Gakkai has created a number of specialized groups or divisions, including those for educators, scientists and academics, artists, writers, and members with international experience and interests, as well as physicians and medical professionals. As the organization has developed a wider range of activities, it has established groups for business professionals, those involved in agriculture and fishing, residents of remote islands, and those involved in community activities and support. It has also founded institutions dedicated to scholarship and the arts such as the Institute of Oriental Philosophy, the Min-On Concert Association, and the Tokyo Fuji Art Museum.

To establish a political movement devoted to serving ordinary people and society in Japan, an independent political party known as Komeito was established in 1964 with the support of Soka Gakkai members.

Sensei also established a system of educational institutions to actualize Makiguchi and Toda's philosophy of value-creating pedagogy, or Soka education. It includes kindergartens; elementary, junior, and senior high schools; and a junior college, universities, and graduate schools. Among these are Tokyo Soka Junior and Senior High Schools (opened in 1968) in Kodaira, Tokyo; Soka University (1971) in Hachioji, Tokyo; and Kansai Soka Junior and Senior High Schools (1973, as Soka Girls' Junior and Senior High Schools) in Katano, Osaka. In 2001, Soka University of America opened in Orange County, California.

At the same time, he was broadening his efforts to conduct dialogues focused on peace, culture, and education on a global scale.

On September 8, 1968, he announced a proposal for the normalization of relations between Japan and China.[13] And beginning in May 1972 he engaged in dialogues with the renowned British historian Arnold J. Toynbee. Their conversations spanned forty hours over a two-year period. This marked the start of a series of dialogues and exchanges with influential leaders and thinkers.

In 1974 and 1975, at the height of the Cold War between the East and West and with China and the Soviet Union also in conflict, Sensei initiated successive visits to China, the Soviet Union, and the United States to engage in talks with their top leaders in order to open paths to peace and friendship.

On January 26, 1975, Soka Gakkai members representing fifty-one countries and territories gathered on the Pacific island of Guam for the establishment of the SGI, appointing Sensei as its president.

Starting from around 1977, as the Soka Gakkai was making great strides toward worldwide kosen-rufu, priests at branch temples of

Nichiren Shoshu began repeatedly making unfounded accusations against the organization. This came to be known as the first priesthood issue. Behind this was an alliance formed of priests and former leaders who had betrayed the Soka Gakkai. They plotted together to sever the bond of mentor and disciple—that is, between Sensei, the leader of the movement for kosen-rufu, and the members—with the goal of controlling the Soka Gakkai for their own aims.

He strove to find a solution to the problem in order to protect the members from these attacks and in hopes of restoring harmony between the priesthood and laity. He found the only feasible way to do so was for him to step down as Soka Gakkai president. In April 1979, he did so, taking the title honorary president.

A Succession of Awards and Honors

Beginning in 1983, Ikeda Sensei issued a peace proposal every year on January 26 in commemoration of SGI Day, the anniversary of the SGI's establishment. These proposals are valued highly by many around the world.

He also delivered more than thirty lectures at universities and academic institutions around the globe, while the number of dialogues he conducted with leading world thinkers, heads of state, cultural figures, and university deans and presidents exceeds sixteen hundred. More than seventy of these dialogues have been published in book form. Among them, the dialogue with Professor Toynbee has been published in some thirty languages, gaining wide praise as a guidepost for global culture and a textbook for humanity.

These dialogues, which connect different cultures and faiths, have helped deepen exchanges among peoples and build mutual understanding and solid bonds among those dedicated to good.

In 1995, the SGI Charter was adopted, making clear the principles of humanism the SGI stands for; and in 1996, the Toda Peace Institute (formerly Toda Institute for Global Peace and Policy Research) was founded, focusing on the legacy of the teachings and principles of Josei Toda.

In response to the SGI's efforts for world peace and activities for culture and education, public parks and streets bearing the names of Presidents Makiguchi, Toda, and Ikeda have appeared in localities throughout the world. Sensei had many honors and awards conferred upon him by nations, municipalities, and educational institutions. These include national medals, honorary doctorates and professorships, and honorary citizenships from numerous cities and counties.

The New Era of Worldwide Kosen-rufu

In the midst of this global progress, in 1991 the Nichiren Shoshu priesthood took the extreme measure of excommunicating millions of Soka Gakkai members throughout the world. This and related events are known as the second priesthood issue. The Soka Gakkai strictly admonished this act perpetrated by a corrupt priesthood, which amounted to a grave slander of Nichiren Daishonin's teachings and betrayal of his intent.

Having triumphed over the schemes of the priesthood, the Soka Gakkai has ushered in a new era in the history of worldwide kosen-rufu. Its members are practicing Nichiren Buddhism in 192 countries and territories, where they have garnered widespread trust and praise for their steady efforts to contribute to society based on the spirit of Buddhist humanism.

In November 2013, the Hall of the Great Vow for Kosen-rufu was completed in Shinanomachi, Tokyo, as part of the Soka Gakkai Headquarters complex.

In his dedication on the monument displayed in the entrance lobby of the Hall of the Great Vow, Sensei wrote: "Kosen-rufu is the path to attaining universal peace and prosperity. It is our great vow from time without beginning for the enlightenment of all people."

Members from across Japan and around the world gather at the Hall of the Great Vow to do gongyo and chant daimoku. United in their vow to achieve kosen-rufu, they pray to the Soka Gakkai Kosen-rufu Gohonzon, which bears the inscription "For the Fulfillment of the Great Vow for Kosen-rufu Through the Compassionate Propagation of the Great Law," and start anew with fresh determination.

Through the efforts of the Soka Gakkai, Nichiren Buddhism now shines as a great source of hope throughout the world, like a sun illuminating all humankind.

NOTES:

1. Translated from Japanese. Tsunesaburo Makiguchi, "Soka kyoikugaku ronshu" [Writings on value-creating education] in *Makiguchi Tsunesaburo zenshu* [The complete works of Tsunesaburo Makiguchi], vol. 8 (Tokyo: Daisanbunmei-sha, 1984), 406.

2. *Makiguchi Tsunesaburo zenshu*, 8:405.

3. State Shinto: a national religion, incorporating native Shinto folk traditions, enlisted as the ideological basis for building the Japanese nation following the Meiji Restoration's reestablishment of imperial rule in 1868. The Meiji Constitution invested the emperor with religious authority and elevated him to the status of an absolute monarch endowed with full sovereign powers. Centering on worship of the Sun Goddess and on the emperor as the absolute authority, the government began totalitarian rule claiming divine authority,

mercilessly exercising its power to promote unity of thought toward spurring the entire country to gear up for war.

4. Peace Preservation Law: Enacted in 1925 and completely revised in 1941, this law was used to suppress thought in the name of protecting the Japanese "national polity" and preserving peace. The law provided for harsh punishment of persons found to be in violation, including the death penalty.

5. Translated from Japanese. Josei Toda, "Makiguchi Sensei sankaiki ni" [On President Makiguchi's third memorial] in *Toda Josei zenshu* [The complete writings of Josei Toda], vol. 3 (Tokyo: Seikyo Shimbun-sha, 1983), 386.

6. The Second Sino-Japanese War: the war that began in 1937 as a Japanese invasion of China and ended with the World War II defeat of Japan in 1945.

7. At the time, the Soka Gakkai's membership was indicated by the number of households.

8. The name Myo Goku derives from Toda's prison experience, during which he had awakened (*go*) to the essence of Buddhism, the mystic truth (*myo*) of nonsubstantiality (*ku*).

9. "Nuclear Weapons" in the title can more literally be translated as "Atomic and Hydrogen Bombs," for this was the common term for nuclear weapons in Japan at that time.

10. Translated from Japanese. Daisaku Ikeda, *Ningen kakumei* [The human revolution], vol. 12 (Tokyo: Seikyo Shimbun-sha, 2013), 490.

11. Ikeda reflects on his choice of Ho Goku as pen name as follows: "Mr. Toda used the pen name Myo Goku; I will use Ho Goku. Combining the first part of each name creates *myoho*, or Mystic Law. *Goku* means to awaken to the truth of nonsubstantiality. The *myo* of *myoho* refers to the world of Buddhahood, and *ho* refers to the other nine worlds. *Myo* is also awakening or enlightenment, while *ho* is fundamental darkness or delusion. Based on this principle we can say that *myo* corresponds to mentor and *ho* to disciple." Translated from Japanese. Daisaku Ikeda, *Shin ningen kakumei* [The new human revolution], vol. 9 (Tokyo: Seikyo Shimbun-sha, 2001), 22.

12. Translated from Japanese. Daisaku Ikeda, *Ningen kakumei* [The human revolution], vol. 1 (Tokyo: Seikyo Shimbun-sha, 2013), 8.

13. At the time, there were no official diplomatic relations between the People's Republic of China and Japan, so technically the two countries were still in a state of war, and anti-China and anticommunist sentiment was widespread in Japan. Ikeda's call for normalization of relations was based on his belief that peace with China was fundamental to the stability of the Asian region and that the reintegration of China into the international community was essential to world peace. His proposal helped establish the groundwork for negotiations leading to the normalization of diplomatic relations in 1972 and a Treaty of Peace and Friendship in 1978.

CHAPTER

11

Learning From Nichiren Daishonin's Writings

"The Wealthy Man Sudatta": Making Offerings in Buddhism

The way to become a Buddha easily is nothing special. It is the same as giving water to a thirsty person in a time of drought, or as providing fire for a person freezing in the cold. Or again, it is the same as giving another something that is one of a kind, or as offering something as alms to another even at the risk of one's life. (WND-1, 1086)

Excerpts from Ikeda Sensei's lecture on this writing in The Teachings for Victory, *vol. 6, pp. 50–51.*

"**The way to** become a Buddha easily is nothing special," Nichiren Daishonin says. First it is providing others with what they need, he writes. For instance, giving water to a thirsty person or providing fire to someone who is freezing. In the bodhisattva practice of almsgiving as well, it is when one provides something that the recipient is truly seeking that the act of almsgiving becomes meaningful. Second, the Daishonin says the way to become a Buddha easily is to offer something that is one of a kind, or something without which one cannot preserve one's own life.

Both of these statements can be interpreted as the highest praise for Nanjo Tokimitsu's sincerity in making an offering to the Daishonin. He is saying that this gift demonstrates that Tokimitsu is already engaged in the practice of becoming a Buddha, walking the path to enlightenment.

People tend to think that attaining Buddhahood requires austere and difficult forms of practice—like that undertaken by the boy Snow Mountains,[1] who was willing to give his most precious possession, his life, for the sake of the Law. But when hearing such stories, ordinary people in the Latter Day become convinced that

TWO TYPES OF OFFERING

The practice of "almsgiving" is one of the six paramitas, or bodhisattva practices. In the Lotus Sutra, Shakyamuni Buddha describes how in a previous existence he was "never stinting in heart" when giving alms, no matter how precious were the goods he gave away (see LSOC, 221).

While there are various types of almsgiving in Buddhism, the two most commonly known are: the offering of goods, providing food and other goods to the Buddha and Buddhist Order; and the offering of the Law, sharing or explaining the Buddha's teachings.

The Daishonin stresses that our contributions, whatever form they take, "implant benefits and roots of goodness" (See "On Attaining Buddhahood in This Lifetime," WND-1, 4) in our lives.

Nichiren and his many disciples exemplified this way of life.

Having gained courage, strength, conviction and hope through faith in Nichiren's such a path is beyond what they can do. Regarding this, Nichiren states, "Ordinary people keep in mind the words 'earnest resolve' [or 'sincere commitment'] and thereby become Buddhas" ("The Gift of Rice," WND-1, 1125).

When we offer something precious and important to us, then in spirit our offering is the same as that of the boy Snow Mountains, who was willing to give his life to a demon [in exchange for hearing an important Buddhist teaching]. For us, this means pledging to carry out kosen-rufu in the course of our daily lives while living life to the fullest. In doing so, we devote our lives to Buddhism and thereby open the life state of Buddhahood within us.

teachings, his disciples, in thanks, provided food, clothing and money to aid in Nichiren's survival and help him further spread his teachings. In turn, Nichiren always expressed his gratitude, never taking anything for granted. Such heart-to-heart exchanges helped both Nichiren and his disciples overcome all adversity.

Today, Soka Gakkai members have inherited Nichiren's spirit to widely spread Buddhism and are overcoming obstacles that attempt to hinder our efforts to develop a wonderful worldwide network of respect and peace. Contributing to others generates the vitality we need to face our challenges. By contributing financially to our movement for kosen-rufu, sharing Buddhism with our friends and family, chanting Nam-myoho-renge-kyo for others, studying Buddhism, and talking with and encouraging one another, we learn how to manifest the same richness of heart as Nichiren. Such efforts sustain, enliven, and strengthen us as we live the vow of a bodhisattva to help all people become happy.

"The True Aspect of All Phenomena": The Two Ways of Practice and Study

Exert yourself in the two ways of practice and study. Without practice and study, there can be no Buddhism. You must not only persevere yourself; you must also teach others. Both practice and study arise from faith. Teach others to the best of your ability, even if it is only a single sentence or phrase. (WND-1, 386)

Excerpts from Ikeda Sensei's lecture in Faith, Practice, and Study, *pp. 51–53.*

Practice and study—which we carry out ourselves and encourage others to do as well—are the heart of Buddhism. In Nichiren Buddhism, it isn't enough that we practice for our own happiness alone. There is no such thing as a selfish Buddha satisfied with attaining personal enlightenment and caring nothing for anyone else. The wisdom of the Buddha exists to lead all people to happiness.

Mr. Makiguchi and Mr. Toda's efforts in practice and study while in prison clearly demonstrate that the Soka Gakkai is directly connected to Nichiren Daishonin. The Soka Gakkai is an organization eternally dedicated to Buddhist study put into action, just as this passage teaches.

The Daishonin continues: "Both practice and study arise from faith. Teach others to the best of your ability, even if it is only a single sentence or phrase." Faith is expressed as concrete efforts in practice and study.

"To the best of your ability" means exerting yourself to the fullest. There is no need to feel hesitant about talking to others about Buddhism because you're not good at Buddhist study. For instance, you could just share some of Nichiren's words that you find moving or something you learned through your Buddhist practice. Or you can tell someone, even with just a few words, that practicing Nichiren Buddhism is enjoyable, that it will enable them to make their wishes come true.

Mr. Toda said:

> Buddhist study in the Soka Gakkai entails reading Nichiren's writings with our deeds, words, and thoughts.[2] As the Daishonin quotes, "The voice carries out the work of the Buddha" (OTT, 4). Please talk with others freely and unhesitatingly about what you've learned about Nichiren Buddhism. By doing so, Buddhist study will eventually become part of your life.

He also said, "Simply attending lectures or reading the Daishonin's writings and saying that one understands the teachings is still the realm of theory; the important thing is to exert oneself in faith and practice in accord with those teachings."

He further stressed to us that actually transforming our lives is more important than mere understanding.

Study based on the mentor-disciple spirit is the Soka Gakkai tradition. It is study for winning, providing us with the foundation to overcome obstacles by learning from Nichiren's conduct and summoning forth the spirit of a lion king. It is study for deepening our faith. It is study for sharing the Mystic Law and realizing kosen-rufu, which spurs us to talk to others about the inspiration and joy we gain from studying the Daishonin's teachings. It is study for inner transformation and human revolution, providing us an opportunity to connect with the Daishonin's heart and confirm that we ourselves embody the Mystic Law.

Practice and study arise from faith, and faith is deepened by pursuing "the two ways of practice and study." This is the rhythm of human revolution and kosen-rufu.

"Happiness in This World": Boundless Joy of the Law

Suffer what there is to suffer, enjoy what there is to enjoy. Regard both suffering and joy as facts of life, and continue chanting Nam-myoho-renge-kyo, no matter what happens. How could this be anything other than the boundless joy of the Law? (WND-1, 681)

Excerpts from Ikeda Sensei's lecture in Learning From the Gosho: The Eternal Teachings of Nichiren Daishonin, *pp. 244–45.*

In times of suffering, chant daimoku. In times of joy, chant daimoku. Chanting daimoku is itself happiness. In life, there are both times of suffering and of joy. These are all irreplaceable scenes in life's drama. Without suffering, we could not appreciate joy. Without tasting the flavors of both suffering and joy, we could not savor life's profundity.

"Suffer what there is to suffer," Nichiren Daishonin says. Suffering is inevitable in life. Therefore, we need to be prepared for hardship and to have the inner fortitude to rise above our worries and anxieties. We have to cause the "tranquil light of the moon of awakening" ("Buddhahood in Its Actual Aspect," WND-2, 892)—the world of Buddhahood—to shine in our lives. Then earthly desires are transformed into enlightenment and we can use everything that happens in life to fuel our happiness.

To "enjoy what there is to enjoy" means to cause "the wonderful lotus that is the inner nature of [our] mind" ("On Forgetting the Copy of the Sutra," WND-2, 659) to brightly blossom with a sense of appreciation and joy. Someone who can find joy, who can feel appreciation, experiences a snowballing exhilaration and joy in life. Such is the heart's function.

The ocean, even when waves are crashing on its surface, is calm and unchanging in its depths. There is both suffering and joy in life—the point is to develop a profound, indomitable self not influenced by these waves. A person who does so receives the joy derived from the Law.

In the journey of kosen-rufu things will not always proceed smoothly. But we are eternal comrades. People who come together in good times but desert one another when the going gets rough are not comrades. Turning a blind eye to the sufferings of others, using the rationale that "it has nothing to do with me," is not the spirit of comrades. True comrades share both suffering and joy.

We suffer together, rejoice together, and bring our lives to fruition together. We regard both suffering and joy as facts of life and continue chanting Nam-myoho-renge-kyo, no matter what happens. To maintain this comradeship, this single-minded commitment to faith, is our eternal guideline in advancing toward kosen-rufu. Let us ever advance with the strong unity of faith!

NOTES:

1. The boy Snow Mountains: The name of Shakyamuni Buddha in a previous lifetime when he was practicing austerities. Deciding to test Snow Mountains' resolve, the god Shakra appeared before him in the form of a hungry demon and recited half a verse from a Buddhist teaching. The boy begged the demon to tell him the second half of the verse. The demon agreed but demanded flesh and blood in payment. Snow Mountains gladly promised to offer his own body to the demon, who in turn gave him the latter half of the teaching. When the boy was about to fulfill his promise, the demon changed back into Shakra and saved him. He praised Snow Mountains for his willingness to give his life for the Law.

2. This refers to the three categories of action; also, three types of action. Activities carried out with one's body, mouth, and mind, i.e., deeds, words, and thoughts. Buddhism holds that karma, good or evil, is created by these three types of action—mental, verbal, and physical. Here, "action" is the translation of the Sanskrit *karman*.

Part 2: Material for Both the Introductory Exam and the Intermediate Exam

CHAPTER

12

Repudiating the Errors of the Nichiren Shoshu Priesthood Under Nikken

Since its establishment, the Soka Gakkai has grounded itself completely on faith that is directly connected to Nichiren Daishonin. It has consistently taken action to spread the Daishonin's Buddhist teachings to create happiness for all people and bring about world peace.

However, a group emerged that sought to destroy this movement for kosen-rufu, and in doing so that group, known as the Nikken sect, revealed its true nature as a devilish function.

The Nikken sect refers to the priesthood of the Nichiren Shoshu Buddhist school in its corrupt state since the tenure of Nikken Abe (1922–2019), who claimed to be the sixty-seventh in the lineage of its high priests. This sect has taken the position that its high priest, who is also its chief administrator, possesses absolute and uncontestable authority and power.

In the three decades since instigating what has become known as the second priesthood issue in 1990, the Nikken sect has betrayed the teachings and spirit of Nichiren Buddhism and has become a group given over to slander of the Buddhist Law.

Though Nikken transferred the office of high priest to Nichinyo in December 2005, the lineage he passed on continues to be muddied by his slander of the Law.

The Battle Against Evil Functions

In his treatise "On Establishing the Correct Teaching for the Peace of the Land," Nichiren Daishonin writes: "Rather than offering up ten thousand prayers for remedy, it would be better simply to outlaw this one evil" (WND-1, 15) and "The only thing to do now is to abandon the evil ways and take up those that are good, to cut off this affliction at the source, to cut it off at the root" (WND-1, 17).

In other words, in striving to practice Buddhism correctly, it is essential to never forget to wage a continuous battle against the one evil, that is, negative influences that delude people and lead them astray.

Speaking Out Against the "Enemies of the Lotus Sutra"

Nichiren Buddhism emphasizes that admonishing and striving against evil is an important element of faith.

The Daishonin writes:

> However great the good causes one may make, or even if one reads and copies the entirety of the Lotus Sutra a thousand or ten thousand times, or attains the way of perceiving three thousand realms in a single moment of life, if one fails to denounce the enemies of the Lotus Sutra, it will be impossible to attain the way. ("Encouragement to a Sick Person," WND-1, 78)

The "enemies of the Lotus Sutra" refers to those who encourage people to abandon the Lotus Sutra and thereby close off the path to Buddhahood for all people.

The Lotus Sutra teaches that the Buddha nature exists in the life of every person, expressing the universal ideal of respect for all human beings. For this reason, to deny or deprecate the sutra, to impede the spread of the sutra, or to oppress or harm practitioners of the sutra is to oppose the ideals of respect for the dignity of life, the equality of all people, and the primacy of ordinary people. To engage in such acts is what it means to become an enemy of the Lotus Sutra.

In light of this, one figure from the Daishonin's lifetime who can be cited as a prime example of an enemy of the Lotus Sutra is Ryokan of Gokuraku-ji temple. While outwardly garnering respect from people of the time, many of whom revered him as a living Buddha, Ryokan covertly harbored animosity toward the Daishonin, who was striving to spread Nam-myoho-renge-kyo, the essence of the Lotus Sutra, and conspired to have him persecuted. In doing so, he functioned as what the Lotus Sutra describes as an arrogant false sage.

In contemporary times, by scheming to destroy the Soka Gakkai, the organization working to accomplish the Daishonin's will of kosen-rufu, it was Nikken who accorded with the definition of an enemy of the Lotus Sutra.

An Overview of the Priesthood Issue

The Daishonin's spirit and practice for kosen-rufu was correctly inherited and carried on by his disciple Nikko Shonin.

That spirit and practice, however, gradually waned within the priesthood of Nichiren Shoshu—a Buddhist school that derived its teachings from the lineage of Nikko Shonin—giving way to hollow formality and ritual. In the process, the priests took on an increasingly authoritarian posture, adopting a discriminatory attitude toward lay believers.

By the time the Soka Gakkai was established, the correct understanding and practice of the Daishonin's teachings had been all but lost within the priesthood.

The Soka Gakkai focused its efforts on realizing the great vow for kosen-rufu and had always supported the priesthood while correcting it whenever necessary.

After World War II, when the priesthood faced severe economic problems, the Soka Gakkai earnestly and sincerely supported and protected it and eventually built and donated more than 350 temples.

However, elements within the priesthood refused to acknowledge or express gratitude for this earnest support, and friction at times arose with certain priests who were intent first on maintaining their religious authority. But in every case, the Soka Gakkai persisted in working to resolve the situation and restore good relations.

The priesthood's tendency to flaunt its authority and look down on lay believers became more pronounced after Nikken took the office of high priest, as it increasingly disregarded the sincere intentions with which the Soka Gakkai had been supporting it for the sake of kosen-rufu.

The Soka Gakkai had been making great strides in establishing Nichiren Buddhism as a world religion, and its leader, Ikeda Sensei had become highly respected among notable world figures in many fields. Nevertheless, Nikken came to regard him with enmity and began plotting to destroy the Soka Gakkai.

Nikken's aim was to sever relations with the Soka Gakkai and take control of its members, turning them into subservient followers of the priests, and in 1990 he conceived and put into action a surreptitious plan he named Operation C ("C" meaning to "cut" the Soka Gakkai).

Its implementation began in December that year with the priesthood's sudden announcement of a revision to its rules as a religious corporation, effectively dismissing Sensei from his position as chief lay representative of Nichiren Shoshu.

The Soka Gakkai sought to address and resolve the situation through dialogue, but the priesthood refused any discussion.

On November 7, 1991, the priesthood sent the Soka Gakkai a document titled "Remonstrance to Disband," followed on November 28 by a "Notice of Excommunication."

In addition to this high-handed move, it took the cruel measure of refusing to confer the Gohonzon upon members of the Soka Gakkai. The priests were telling people, in effect, that if they wished to receive the Gohonzon, they could do so only by following the priesthood. In this way, they were holding the Gohonzon, the basis of faith, hostage in a cowardly attempt to pressure and intimidate believers.

Nevertheless, in 1993 the Soka Gakkai decided that it would confer upon its members around the world a Gohonzon transcribed by Nichikan Shonin, a great restorer of Nichiren Buddhism. This was made possible through the cooperation of a temple that had opposed Nikken's actions and supported the Soka Gakkai.

The Soka Gakkai is now the only religious group working to achieve kosen-rufu in direct accord with Nichiren Daishonin's spirit, conferring upon believers the Gohonzon, which he described as "the banner of propagation of the Lotus Sutra" ("The Real Aspect of the Gohonzon," WND-1, 831). As such, the Soka Gakkai has become the global organization qualified to confer the Gohonzon in order to realize kosen-rufu, the Buddha's will and intent.

In 1998, the Nikken sect demolished the Grand Main Temple, an edifice at the Nichiren Shoshu head temple, Taiseki-ji, built in 1972 under the aegis of the Soka Gakkai through the sincere faith and contributions of some eight million people. This reckless act made the priesthood's malicious and vindictive nature all the more apparent.

The Grand Main Temple, constructed to last one thousand years, was hailed as a masterpiece of twentieth-century architecture that rivaled any religious edifice in the world. Nikken, however, heartlessly had it demolished just twenty-six years after its completion, disregarding the sincere faith of eight million believers.

The Major Offenses and Erroneous Doctrines of the Nikken Sect

Core to the Nikken sect is a deluded belief that venerates its high priest as a special, absolute, and infallible being, a belief that might be called high priest worship. One of the premises for this claim is that there exists a mysterious heritage, or lineage, that is passed on only from one high priest to the next, a presumption that bolstered the priesthood's tendency to look down on lay believers.

Of course, there is nothing in Nichiren Daishonin's writings to justify or support this in any way, and it therefore constitutes a false doctrine that is starkly opposed to the teachings of Nichiren Buddhism.

Careful study of the essential principles of Nichiren Buddhism makes clear the key errors of the Nikken sect.

1. The Slander of Attempting to Destroy Kosen-rufu

The Nikken sect implemented its Operation C with the aim of destroying the Soka Gakkai, the organization dedicated to kosen-rufu, and in 1991 it sent the Soka Gakkai its notice of excommunication.

The document cited no passages from Nichiren Daishonin's writings and expressed no doctrinal basis to support the Soka Gakkai's excommunication. It simply asserted in an authoritarian and emotional manner that the Soka Gakkai was not obediently following the priesthood.

The task of achieving kosen-rufu, the widespread propagation of the Mystic Law, is the legacy left by Nichiren Daishonin. This is evident when he declares: "The 'great vow' refers to the propagation of the Lotus Sutra" (OTT, 82) and "When you are so united, even the great desire for widespread propagation can be fulfilled" ("The Heritage of the Ultimate Law of Life," WND-1, 217).

It is for this reason that the Soka Gakkai has aimed since its founding to accomplish kosen-rufu, exerting itself in the propagation of Nichiren Buddhism not only in Japan but throughout the world.

To attempt to destroy the Soka Gakkai, therefore, is to attempt to destroy kosen-rufu, an act that constitutes a grave slander of the Buddhist Law and the great offense of betraying the Daishonin's spirit and intent to save all people from suffering.

Nikken's Grave Offense of Causing Disunity in the Buddhist Order

The Buddhist teachings describe the greatest offenses a person can commit as the "five cardinal sins."

These are (1) killing one's father, (2) killing one's mother, (3) killing an arhat, (4) injuring a Buddha, and (5) causing disunity in the Buddhist Order.

Among these offenses, causing disunity in the Buddhist Order, or actions that create disruption and division among the body of Buddhist practitioners, is extremely serious as it destroys the Buddha's teachings and deludes people, causing them to fall into unhappiness. This is the gravest offense that Nikken committed.

2. The False Doctrine of Worship of the High Priest

It is the doctrine of the Nikken sect that the high priest be regarded as an object of worship or veneration. A high priest should be a person who is primarily responsible for protecting, teaching, and spreading the Buddhist teachings. This person should serve as a model for carrying out faith, practice, and study and for upholding the correct teachings.

In this regard, since the outbreak of the second priesthood issue, Nikken and his supporters, rejecting any dialogue, consistently claimed that because the high priest is infallible and an object of worship or veneration, one must follow him without question.

The idea of the high priest as an object of faith is an extremely vain doctrine that violates the three treasures—the Buddha, the Law (the Buddha's teachings), and the Buddhist Order—of Nichiren Buddhism.

For example, a document[1] carried in a Nichiren Shoshu publication states that the high priest to whom the heritage of the Law has been transmitted is an honorable entity that is one and inseparable with the Dai-Gohonzon[2] and that faith in these two fundamental objects (the Dai-Gohonzon and the high priest) must be absolute.

In Nichiren Buddhism, however, there is just one object of devotion, the Gohonzon.

The Nikken sect's erroneous doctrine purports that the high priest, whose function should be to protect the Gohonzon, instead stands on an equal par with the Gohonzon. This is a dogma of unprecedented distortion.

Correct Faith Means Basing Oneself on the Gohonzon

Since the time of the Daishonin and Nikko Shonin, correct faith has been defined as faith based upon the Gohonzon.

Nichiren Daishonin writes: "Believe in this mandala with all your heart" ("Reply to Kyo'o," WND-1, 412) and "Since Nichiren's disciples and lay supporters believe solely in the Lotus Sutra . . . they can enter the treasure tower of the Gohonzon" ("The Real Aspect of the Gohonzon," WND-1, 832).

And Nikko Shonin states, "It is specified in the honorable writings [of Nichiren Daishonin] that the five characters of Myoho-renge-kyo should be the object of devotion. That is, the object of devotion he inscribed in his own hand" (GZ, new ed., 2180; GZ, 1606).

The Error of Regarding the High Priest as Infallible

In Twenty-Six Admonitions of Nikko,[3] he writes, "Do not follow even the high priest if he goes against the Buddha's Law and propounds his own views" (GZ, new ed., 2196; GZ, 1618).

Nikko Shonin issued this warning based on his assumption that it was possible that in the future the head of the school might commit a serious error.

In the same document, Nikko Shonin writes:

> My disciples should conduct themselves as holy priests, patterning their behavior after that of the late master. However, even if a high priest or a priest striving for practice and understanding should temporarily deviate from the principle of sexual abstinence, he may still be allowed to remain in the priesthood as a common priest without rank. (GZ, new ed., 2197; GZ, 1619)

This means that if a high priest or a senior priest of considerable learning should commit a prohibited act or serious error that by rights would warrant expulsion, he should rather be allowed to renew his practice among priests of ordinary rank while pursuing a basic path of reflection and contrition.

From these admonitions of Nikko Shonin, it is clear that the view that the high priest is infallible promoted by the Nikken sect is completely misguided. It is a dogma that violates the teachings of both the Daishonin and Nikko Shonin.

3. A Mistaken View of Heritage

Heritage, or lineage, in Nichiren Buddhism has always been something open to all people, not the exclusive possession of an elite few. However, Nikken and his followers held an erroneous view of heritage that is the source of their notion that the high priest is absolute.

That view is as follows: There exists a mysterious heritage or lineage that is passed on only from one high priest to the next. Simply by receiving that lineage, one exclusively inherits the Buddha's enlightenment and the essence of the Buddha's Law itself.

In the same document carried in a Nichiren Shoshu publication cited earlier, the Nikken sect states that the transmission of the heritage of the Law entrusted to only one person is surely the entity that embodies the oneness of the Person and the Law.

The idea of such a mysterious transmission is an erroneous doctrine that bears no relation to the teachings of the Daishonin or Nikko Shonin. It amounts to a falsehood concocted in later times to bolster the status and authority of the high priest.

The True Meaning of Heritage Is Faith That Is Open to All People

The Japanese term for heritage, literally "bloodline," is used frequently in the esoteric teachings of the True Word school and by schools such as Tendai and Zen. It likens the transfer of the teachings from teacher to disciple to the genetic heritage passed from parent to child.

In the Buddhist world of Nichiren Daishonin's time, this heritage predominantly meant the passing on of the deepest Buddhist teachings to a select group of individuals in the form of a secret transmission.

In contrast to this, in "The Heritage of the Ultimate Law of Life," the Daishonin writes, "Nichiren has been trying to awaken all the people of Japan to faith in the Lotus Sutra so that they too can share the heritage and attain Buddhahood" (WND-1, 217).

In Nichiren Buddhism, the heritage is ultimately described as the "heritage of faith" (WND-1, 218), that is, as faith itself.

On the other hand, the Nikken sect claims a mysterious, exclusive heritage that upon receipt automatically makes one a Buddha regardless of faith or practice. This is far removed from the essential meaning of the heritage of faith, the heritage taught by the Daishonin.

4. Discriminatory Attitude Toward the Laity

An idea that permeates the entire Nichiren Shoshu priesthood, from Nikken to all the priests, is that they as priests are superior and that lay believers are inferior. That is, they adopt a discriminatory attitude toward the laity.

There is no teaching or principle within Nichiren Buddhism that would justify priests treating laypeople with such disrespect or contempt.

On the contrary, the Daishonin clearly confirmed the equality of clergy and laity, saying: "For this reason, the Buddha surely considers anyone in this world who embraces the Lotus Sutra, whether lay man or woman, monk or nun, to be the lord of all living beings" ("The Unity of Husband and Wife," WND-1, 463) and "Anyone who teaches others even a single phrase of the Lotus Sutra is the envoy of the Thus Come One, whether that person be priest or layman, nun or laywoman" ("A Ship to Cross the Sea of Suffering," WND-1, 33).

Behind the Nikken sect's blatant denial of the equality of clergy and laity is the degradation of the role of Buddhism in Japan, primarily during the Edo period (1603–1867), to the extent that it became known as funeral Buddhism, and the spread of the so-called temple parishioner system[4] during the same period. This resulted in priests exerting control over lay believers and forcing them into a servile position, while lay believers came to depend entirely on the priests rather than carry out their own Buddhist practice.

The harmful tendencies and errors inherent in the temple parishioner system remain deeply ingrained in the Nikken sect, and this has resulted in a belief that priests are superior to laity.

5. Misuse of Religious Rituals

One of the major errors of the Nikken sect is its misuse of Buddhist rituals and ceremonies, turning them into means for making money. These include funeral and memorial services, the bestowal of posthumous Buddhist names, and the issuing of wooden memorial tablets to be placed beside the grave.

Such rituals conducted by priests today were not instituted by the Daishonin but became established in later times. The Nikken sect asserts that unless a funeral service is conducted by a priest, the deceased will be unable to attain Buddhahood; but the Daishonin never taught or stated anything of the sort.

Rather, he encouraged those who had lost loved ones with such statements as "Therefore, because your beloved departed father chanted Nam-myoho-renge-kyo while he was alive, he was a person who attained Buddhahood in his present form" ("White Horses and White Swans," WND-1, 1064).

In this way, he stressed that attaining Buddhahood depends on one's faith and practice while alive.

Therefore, to ignore the Daishonin's guidance and assert that the deceased cannot attain Buddhahood unless a priest conducts their funeral in itself constitutes the offense of distorting the Daishonin's teachings.

6. Corruption and Immorality

With regard to the conduct of priests, Nichiren Daishonin states, "True priests are those who are honest and who desire little and yet know satisfaction" ("The Essentials for Attaining Buddhahood," WND-1, 747).

The priests of the Nikken sect, however, beginning with Nikken himself, have consistently behaved in a corrupt and self-indulgent manner in stark violation of the Daishonin's instruction. The Daishonin compared any such irresponsible priest who uses Buddhism for selfish gain to "an animal dressed in priestly robes" ("The Fourteen Slanders," WND-1, 760) or to "Law-devouring hungry spirits" ("The Origin of the Service for Deceased Ancestors," WND-1, 191).

Spiritual Independence

November 28, 1991, marked the day that the Soka Gakkai was excommunicated from Nichiren Shoshu. To Soka Gakkai members, however, this day marks the day they achieved their spiritual independence. Freeing themselves from the chains of the corrupt and misguided priesthood, Soka Gakkai members have emerged all around the globe, embracing their mission to achieve kosen-rufu. Their numbers have steadily grown, and today they are active in 192 countries and territories worldwide.

The Nikken sect, on the other hand, has continued on its course of decline, its membership today a mere 2 percent of what it was before it excommunicated the Soka Gakkai.

By striving to achieve the Daishonin's will for kosen-rufu, the Soka Gakkai has succeeded to the true heritage of Nichiren Buddhism. Resolutely challenging and refuting the false and destructive actions of the Nikken sect, Soka Gakkai members are opening the way for the further expansion of kosen-rufu throughout the world.

NOTES:

1. The document in question was coauthored by several Nichiren Shoshu senior priests in July 1991 and reprinted in the September 1991 issue of the Nichiren Shoshu publication *Dainichiren.*

2. Dai-Gohonzon, also known as the Gohonzon inscribed in the second year of the Koan era (1279), is a wooden mandala that Nichiren Shoshu considers its fundamental and sole object of devotion. In the past, for the sake of kosen-rufu, the Soka Gakkai strove for harmonious unity with the priests and accepted its doctrine regarding this Gohonzon. The priests, however, began to use their possession of this mandala to claim their superiority and authority over all lay believers, as well as the infallibility of their high priest. Nichiren never identified a particular Gohonzon as superior, or as possessing special powers beyond the faith and practice of ordinary believers. Therefore, the Soka Gakkai today does not regard this Gohonzon as being superior to any other Gohonzon. It also refutes Nichiren Shoshu's assertion that all other Gohonzon gain efficacy only through a link to this particular wooden mandala.

3. "The Twenty-six Admonitions of Nikko"was written by Nikko Shonin in 1333 and addresses practitioners of future generations, exhorting them to maintain the purity of Nichiren's teachings, and outlines the fundamental spirit of faith, practice, and study.

4. The temple parishioner system: A means by which families were affiliated officially with a local Buddhist temple during the regime of the Tokugawa Shogunate (1603–1867). It was a mandatory system of citizen registration intended to detect hidden Christians—those secretly practicing Christianity, which had been outlawed. It was also a way for the government, with the temples as proxies, to monitor and control the population. Under the system, individuals and families were not permitted to change religious affiliation. People were expected to visit their assigned temple and rely on it to conduct funeral and memorial ceremonies, to offer donations for these services, and thereby provide the temples with a permanent source of income.

Part 3: Material for the Intermediate Exam

CHAPTER

13

Nichiren Daishonin and the Lotus Sutra

The Lotus Sutra

The **Lotus Sutra** is a scripture that embodies the essence of Mahayana Buddhism. It teaches unequivocally that all people can attain Buddhahood. This section will explain the significance and major doctrines of the Lotus Sutra.

The Lotus Sutra has radically changed the Buddhist view of life and of Buddhahood. The sutras Shakyamuni preached during the more than forty years before the Lotus Sutra teach that ordinary people cannot attain Buddhahood in this lifetime. Moreover, they stay in one of nine worlds other than Buddhahood until they die and only then can move to another in rebirth. Therefore, if people wish to attain Buddhahood, they have to carry out Buddhist practices through numerous lifetimes until they eradicate all of their earthly desires, purify their lives, and obtain benefit and virtue worthy of Buddhas. Then and only then can they attain Buddhahood. And when they succeed, only the world of Buddhahood will be present in their lives.

However, in the Lotus Sutra Shakyamuni reveals the truth that Buddhahood exists inherently in the lives of ordinary people and that everyone can attain Buddhahood immediately by bringing it forth from within their lives.

This teaching of the Lotus Sutra is founded on two doctrines: the true aspect of all phenomena and the attainment of Buddhahood in the remote past.

The True Aspect of All Phenomena and the Attainment of Buddhahood in the Remote Past

The True Aspect of All Phenomena

The Lotus Sutra, which consists of twenty-eight chapters, can be divided into two distinct parts: the theoretical teaching, which equates to the first fourteen chapters, and the essential teaching, the latter fourteen chapters.

Two doctrines central to the theoretical teaching (the first half) are the true aspect of all phenomena and the attainment of Buddhahood by people of the two vehicles.

The true aspect of all phenomena is a principle expounded in "Expedient Means," the second chapter. *All phenomena* here means the world around us and its various workings, including the affairs of life and society. *True aspect* means their ultimate reality or true essential nature.

The truth or reality of all things that Buddhas, through their vast and profound wisdom, are able to perceive is called the true aspect of all phenomena. Once one perceives this reality, one understands that all phenomena and their true aspect are not two separate things but that all phenomena are in fact manifestations or expressions of the true aspect. Therefore, all phenomena and their true aspect can never be divided or separated.

Based on the commentaries of Great Teacher T'ien-t'ai (Zhiyi), Nichiren Daishonin clarified that all phenomena refers specifically to all living beings of the Ten Worlds and their respective environments, whereas the true aspect refers to Myoho-renge-kyo.

In his work "The True Aspect of All Phenomena," the Daishonin states that "all beings and environments in the Ten Worlds, from hell, the lowest, to Buddhahood, the highest, are without exception manifestations of Myoho-renge-kyo" (WND-1, 383).

The teaching of the true aspect of all phenomena reveals that not only Buddhas but also the beings of the other nine worlds are all equal because each of the Ten Worlds possesses all of the ten and are essentially embodiments of Myoho-renge-kyo.

Prior to the Lotus Sutra, it was thought that a practically insurmountable gap lay between a Buddha and an ordinary person; that is, between the life state of Buddhahood and the other nine worlds.

However, the Lotus Sutra takes the opposite view. While Buddhas and ordinary people of the nine worlds take on different appearances and qualities in terms of their roles and behavior in the real world, on the level of life itself they are essentially the same, with no distinction between them. Beings of the nine worlds, whatever their present condition or state of life, are all in principle capable of attaining Buddhahood.

Based on the principle of the true aspect of all phenomena, the Lotus Sutra reveals that people of the two vehicles (voice-hearers and cause-awakened ones) can in fact become Buddhas, although the pre-Lotus Sutra teachings denied their possibility of attaining Buddhahood.

Furthermore, the Lotus Sutra also guarantees the attainment of Buddhahood by evil people as well as the attainment of Buddhahood by women—two groups that were also denied the possibility of enlightenment in the pre-Lotus Sutra teachings.

The "Expedient Means" chapter goes on to explain that the reason or purpose for which all Buddhas appear in this world is to "open the door of Buddha wisdom" for all people, to "show the Buddha wisdom" to them, to "cause them to awaken to the Buddha wisdom" and to "induce [them] to enter the path of Buddha wisdom" (LSOC, 64).

In other words, the fundamental wish of Shakyamuni and all other Buddhas is to enable all people to reveal the Buddha wisdom, inherent equally in everyone's life, and to carry out Buddhist practice based on that wisdom. In this way, they aim to enable all people to achieve a state of life equal to that of the Buddhas themselves. This is conveyed in the Lotus Sutra by Shakyamuni's statement of his long-held vow "to make all persons equal to me, without any distinction between us" (LSOC, 70). This is the fundamental purpose of Buddhism.

The Attainment of Buddhahood in the Remote Past

A principle central to the essential teaching (the latter half) of the Lotus Sutra is the revelation of Shakyamuni's attainment of Buddhahood in the remote past.

In the pre-Lotus Sutra teachings up through the theoretical teaching (the first half) of the Lotus Sutra, Shakyamuni is described as follows: He was born a prince of the country of the Shakya clan in ancient India but left home to pursue a religious life and after a period of ascetic practices attained enlightenment, or Buddhahood, for the first time while seated in meditation under the Bodhi tree on the outskirts of Gaya (later called Bodh Gaya). According to those teachings, the causes he had made and accumulated through many lifetimes of Buddhist practice had resulted in his obtaining the rewards of benefit and virtue that enabled him, in his present life in India, to attain Buddhahood.

But his revelation that he had actually attained enlightenment in the distant past fundamentally overturned that existing image.

As explained earlier, the teaching of the true aspect of all phenomena in the theoretical teaching reveals that there is no essential difference between a Buddha and an ordinary person, because both are embodiments of Myoho-renge-kyo. In other words, while Buddhahood is inherent in the lives of ordinary people and anyone can attain Buddhahood at any time, it would actually require practice over numerous lifetimes to do so. In the theoretical teaching, even Shakyamuni is seen as having attained Buddhahood only after an unimaginably long period of practice, and so disciples would naturally have to carry out the same practice as their teacher.

In contrast, the essential teaching, through the example of Shakyamuni attaining enlightenment in the remote past, explains that Buddhahood, along with the other nine worlds, is permanently inherent in the lives of all people and that they can manifest Buddhahood at any moment under the right conditions.

"Life Span," the sixteenth chapter, offers a description of a period known as "numberless major world system dust particle kalpas" to explain the vastness of the time that has passed since Shakyamuni originally attained Buddhahood. This overturned the accepted view that Shakyamuni had attained enlightenment for the first time during his lifetime in India and revealed him to be the eternal Buddha who had been enlightened since the remote past. It also explains that since that time he has always been present in this impure saha world.[1]

The chapter says, "It has been immeasurable, boundless hundreds, thousands, ten thousands, millions of nayutas of kalpas since I in fact attained Buddhahood" (LSOC, 265–66). This signifies that the life state of the Buddha is eternal and always present.

After revealing his original enlightenment in the remote past, Shakyamuni states, "Originally I practiced the bodhisattva way, and the life span that I acquired then has yet to come to an end but will last twice the number of years that have already passed" (LSOC, 268). This means that the nine worlds, represented by the life state of a bodhisattva, are also eternal and always present.

The above two passages mean that both the life state of Buddhahood and that of the nine worlds are forever present in Shakyamuni's life.

Before the Lotus Sutra clarified that Shakyamuni had attained

Buddhahood in the remote past, it was taught that before becoming a Buddha in India he had purged the nine worlds and their delusions from his life.

In contrast, Shakyamuni's revelation of his original enlightenment shows that all of the other nine worlds are inherent within the world of Buddhahood in his life. Therefore, he was able to appear as a bodhisattva taking various forms as he carried out Buddhist practice in subsequent lifetimes in the past. But even while appearing and acting as a bodhisattva, Buddhahood always existed within his life. In this way he embodied the "mutual possession of the Ten Worlds."

Shakyamuni, the Buddha who attained enlightenment in the remote past, is in fact free from the endless cycle of birth and death, but in order to cause people to seek his teachings, he passes away. He states in the "Life Span" chapter, "As an expedient means I appear to enter nirvana but in truth I do not pass into extinction" (LSOC, 270–71).

Further, the sutra explains that this eternal Buddha always dwells in the Land of Eternally Tranquil Light, which is none other than this saha world where ordinary people of the nine worlds live. (This is known as the principle that the saha world is the Land of Eternally Tranquil Light.) He appears whenever and wherever there are people who seek the Buddha single-mindedly and strive in Buddhist practice without begrudging their lives.

In other words, when one believes in and practices the Lotus Sutra, one's innate Buddhahood emerges, and at the same time, one's environment becomes a Buddha land. This is because everyone's life is inherently endowed with the state of a Buddha. This innate Buddha nature functions as the internal cause, which in response to the right conditions brings about, at any time or any place, the reward of Buddhahood in one's own being and in the environment.

It is the principle of Shakyamuni's attainment of Buddhahood in the remote past that sheds light on the true nature of life; namely that from the most distant past into the limitless future, everyone is essentially a Buddha.

The Bodhisattvas of the Earth

In "Emerging from the Earth," the fifteenth chapter of the Lotus Sutra, Shakyamuni summons countless bodhisattvas for the purpose of entrusting them with the propagation of his teaching in the evil age after his passing. Because the sutra depicts them as emerging in vast numbers from beneath the ground, they are known as the Bodhisattvas of the Earth and are considered to have been dwelling in the realm of fundamental truth.

The Bodhisattvas of the Earth are countless in number, each leading an entourage of followers as numerous as the sands of sixty thousand Ganges, the greatest and most venerated river in India.

These bodhisattvas had been constantly taught and instructed by Shakyamuni since the remote past and had already come to uphold the fundamental teaching for attaining Buddhahood. Possessing within them the same enlightened life state as Shakyamuni, they are charged with the mission to widely spread the Mystic Law in the evil age known as the Latter Day of the Law.

They are led by four bodhisattvas—Superior Practices, Boundless Practices, Pure Practices, and Firmly Established Practices. In "Supernatural Powers," the twenty-first chapter of the Lotus Sutra, Superior Practices and all these bodhisattvas vow to spread the great Law after Shakyamuni's passing. In response to their vow, Shakyamuni entrusts them with propagating his teaching in the age after his passing, charging them with transmitting the great Law into the future.

In view of these sutra passages, two major questions still remain. That is, when after Shakyamuni's passing will the Bodhisattvas of the Earth actually appear, and what exactly is the great Law they will spread when they do?

Nichiren Daishonin makes it clear that the time when the Bodhisattvas of the Earth will appear is in the Latter Day of the Law, and the great Law they will spread is the Mystic Law, or Nam-myoho-renge-kyo.

The Daishonin himself fulfilled the instructions contained in this entrustment of the teachings by Shakyamuni described in the Lotus Sutra. That is, it is the Daishonin who appeared at the beginning of the Latter Day of the Law, taught Nam-myoho-renge-kyo to all people, and spread it with selfless dedication. In this sense, the Daishonin is himself a Bodhisattva of the Earth, whose role accords in particular with that of their leader, Bodhisattva Superior Practices.

In "The True Aspect of All Phenomena," Nichiren Daishonin writes:

> Now, no matter what, strive in faith and be known as a votary of the Lotus Sutra, and remain my disciple for the rest of your life. If you are of the same mind as Nichiren, you must be a Bodhisattva of the Earth. And if you are a Bodhisattva of the Earth, there is not the slightest doubt that you have been a disciple of Shakyamuni Buddha from the remote past. (WND-1, 385)

This passage explains that everyone who accepts and believes in the Daishonin's teachings, propagates them, and works to achieve kosen-rufu is without exception a Bodhisattva of the Earth. That person is a genuine disciple of Nichiren Daishonin, the Buddha of the Latter Day of the Law.

Bodhisattva Never Disparaging

The practice of Bodhisattva Never Disparaging described in "Never Disparaging," the twentieth chapter of the Lotus Sutra, serves as an example of how to spread the correct teaching in the evil age after Shakyamuni's passing.

Never Disparaging is one of the figures appearing in the Lotus Sutra who depicts Shakyamuni as he carried out Buddhist practices in a former lifetime. He consistently venerates everyone he encounters, no matter who they are, including even those who attack or persecute him, bowing in respect and reciting to each a phrase known as the twenty-four-character Lotus Sutra. This name derives from the fact that the phrase consists of twenty-four Chinese characters in the sutra's text and expresses the essence of the Lotus Sutra's teachings and practice. It reads:

> I have profound reverence for you, I would never dare treat you with disparagement or arrogance. Why? Because you will all practice the bodhisattva way and will then be able to attain Buddhahood. (LSOC, 308)

These words plainly demonstrate the Lotus Sutra's essential philosophy, which is to respect the life of any and every person because each inherently possesses the Buddha nature.

While preaching this twenty-four-character Lotus Sutra, Never Disparaging is attacked by arrogant people who throw rocks and hit him with sticks, but he perseveres in his practice of consistently praising them and treating them with respect. The sutra explains that it was through the benefit deriving from these actions that Never Disparaging became a Buddha.

The Latter Day of the Law is described as an age of contention or conflict. And the only way to resolve conflict and create a society of humanity and peace is for each person to believe in the Buddha nature of both themselves and others, and to consistently act in a manner that shows respect for people. Buddhism teaches the loftiest form of human behavior—actions that respect others—and encourages all people to act in this manner.

Regarding the importance of human behavior, Nichiren states:

> The heart of the Buddha's lifetime of teachings is the Lotus Sutra, and the heart of the practice of the Lotus Sutra is found in the "Never Disparaging" chapter. What does Bodhisattva Never Disparaging's profound respect for people signify? The purpose of the appearance in this world of Shakyamuni Buddha, the lord of teachings, lies in his behavior as a human being. ("The Three Kinds of Treasure," WND-1, 851–52)

Here the Daishonin is clearly stating that the purpose of Buddhism is to behave as Never Disparaging did, that is, to believe in one's own Buddha nature and that of others and act in accord with that belief.

Nichiren Daishonin and the Lotus Sutra

In the Latter Day of Law, it is inevitable that those who spread the Lotus Sutra will encounter great difficulties. Nichiren Daishonin propagated the Lotus Sutra and encountered major persecutions for doing so, just as the sutra predicted. In this way, he "read" the Lotus Sutra with his very life and fulfilled the role of the votary of the Lotus Sutra who proves the validity of the sutra's teachings.

The Votary of the Lotus Sutra in the Latter Day of the Law

Nichiren Daishonin referred to himself as the votary of the Lotus Sutra—the genuine practitioner of the sutra who carried out its teachings exactly as instructed while facing and overcoming great persecutions in order to propagate the Mystic Law. The Lotus Sutra explains that anyone who believes in, practices, and spreads the sutra's teaching after Shakyamuni's passing will be assailed by various kinds of obstacles and persecutions.

Suffering Extreme Hatred and Jealousy

In "Teacher of the Law," the tenth chapter of the Lotus Sutra, is the passage "Since hatred and jealousy toward this sutra abound even when the thus come one [Shakyamuni Buddha] is in the world, how much more will this be so after his passing?" (LSOC, 203)

In the Latter Day of the Law, it was only Nichiren Daishonin who experienced persecutions motived by intense hatred and jealously surpassing those directed at Shakyamuni in his time.

The Six Difficult and Nine Easy Acts

"Emergence of the Treasure Tower," the eleventh chapter of the Lotus Sutra, describes six difficult and nine easy acts. Through these examples, Shakyamuni emphasizes the great difficulty of accepting and spreading the Lotus Sutra in the time after his passing and calls on bodhisattvas to make a vow to propagate the sutra in the Latter Day of the Law.

The six difficult acts are (1) to propagate the Lotus Sutra widely, (2) to copy it or cause someone else to copy it, (3) to recite it even for a short while, (4) to teach it even to one person, (5) to hear of and accept it and inquire about its meaning, and (6) to maintain faith in it.

The nine easy acts include taking up Mount Sumeru and hurling it across countless Buddha lands, placing the earth on one's toenail and ascending to the Brahma heaven, walking across a burning prairie carrying a bundle of hay on one's back without being burned, and preaching eighty-four thousand teachings.

While the nine "easy" acts appear impossible, they are considered easy when compared with the difficulty of the six acts connected with spreading the Lotus Sutra in the Latter Day of the Law.

The reason that propagating the Lotus Sutra is so difficult is that doing so invites very real hardships in the form of opposition and persecution. In explaining things in terms of the six difficult and nine easy acts, the sutra is strongly expressing Shakyamuni's spirit and intent in encouraging the propagation of its teachings, the most difficult among difficult endeavors, in the age after his passing.

The Three Powerful Enemies

"Encouraging Devotion," the thirteenth chapter of the Lotus Sutra, contains a passage known as the twenty-line verse[2] describing three kinds of people who strongly oppress those who spread the sutra after Shakyamuni's passing. Collectively, they are called the "three powerful enemies." They are defined as arrogant laypeople, arrogant priests, and arrogant false sages.

The first of the three powerful enemies, arrogant laypeople, refers to people who, ignorant of the Buddhist teachings, attack the practitioners of the Lotus Sutra. Because the Daishonin endeavored to spread the Lotus Sutra, such people slandered him and attacked him with swords and staves, just as the sutra predicted.

The second powerful enemy, arrogant priests, indicates members of the Buddhist clergy who persecute the Lotus Sutra's practitioners. In the Daishonin's time, Buddhist priests, clinging to their own shallow views and interpretations, slandered the sutra and persecuted him.

The third powerful enemy, arrogant false sages, refers to high-ranking Buddhist priests who pass themselves off as sages or saints and use their status and influence to persecute the practitioners of the Lotus Sutra.

During the Daishonin's time, the priest Ryokan of Gokuraku-ji temple best fit this description of an arrogant false sage. While he was highly respected as a saint by the people of Kamakura, he was in reality most concerned with personal profit and advantage and maliciously sought to destroy the votary of the Lotus Sutra. He ingratiated himself with the wives of certain government officials, among whom he spread rumors and false accusations against Nichiren Daishonin and his followers, plotting in this way to influence the authorities to oppress the Daishonin. This led to the Daishonin's persecution at Tatsunokuchi—a failed attempt to execute him—and his subsequent exile to Sado Island.

Because he was sent into exile twice—first to Ito on the Izu Peninsula and second to Sado Island—Nichiren Daishonin stated that he had read with his very life the passage in the "Encouraging Devotion" chapter that reads "again and again we will be banished" (LSOC, 234).

It is clear, then, that Nichiren Daishonin encountered major persecutions at the hands of the three powerful enemies, exactly as the Lotus Sutra says will befall its votary, or true practitioner. Because he met persecutions on account of propagating the Lotus Sutra that exactly matched those predicted in the sutra itself, the Daishonin, in "The Selection of the Time," writes, "There can be no room to doubt that I, Nichiren, am the foremost votary of the Lotus Sutra in all of Japan" (WND-1, 575). In the same work, he also states, "I, Nichiren, am the foremost votary of the Lotus Sutra in the entire land of Jambudvipa [the entire world]" (WND-1, 552).

In light of all this, the Lotus Sutra is the Buddhist scripture that predicts the Daishonin's appearance and behavior in the Latter Day of the Law, and by reading the Lotus Sutra with his very life (by fulfilling the predictions made in the sutra), the Daishonin proved that the sutra itself was in no way false, attesting to the validity of Shakyamuni's words.

Bodhisattva Superior Practices

Nichiren Daishonin was the first to stand alone and stake his life on spreading the Mystic Law as the votary of the Lotus Sutra in the Latter Day of the Law. In this way, he demonstrated that his mission and behavior accorded with that of Bodhisattva Superior Practices, whom Shakyamuni, in the Lotus Sutra, entrusted with propagating the sutra's teaching in the Latter Day of the Law.

The "Supernatural Powers" chapter explains that having been entrusted with propagating the sutra's teaching in the Latter Day of the Law, Superior Practices and the other Bodhisattvas of the Earth will function as the sun and moon to illuminate and expel the obscurity and gloom plaguing people living amid the realities of this world. Also, in the "Emerging from the Earth" chapter, the Bodhisattvas of the Earth are compared to the lotus flowers that, unsullied by this impure world and untroubled by earthly desires or afflictions, blossom and bring forth the fruit of enlightenment.

This indicates that Superior Practices is the enlightened teacher of the Latter Day of the Law who in Shakyamuni's stead teaches and leads the people of this age to Buddhahood.

Nichiren Daishonin gave himself the name Nichiren (meaning sun lotus) and as the votary of the Lotus Sutra persevered in his efforts to save people from suffering. His choice of this name expresses his conviction that he is fulfilling the role of Superior Practices, whose function is compared in the "Supernatural Powers" and "Emerging from the Earth" chapters to the sun, the moon, and the lotus flower.

While in terms of his behavior the Daishonin was carrying out the function of Superior Practices, on a deeper level—in terms of his intrinsic, enlightened state of life—he was the Buddha of limitless joy from time without beginning, the Buddha who can fully display the dignity life inherently possesses.

The Daishonin expressed this fundamental life state of Buddhahood in the form of a mandala, the Gohonzon, which he modeled after the Ceremony in the Air[3] in the Lotus Sutra, establishing it as the object of devotion that all people of the Latter Day of the Law should believe in and uphold in order to attain Buddhahood.

When one believes in the Gohonzon of Nam-myoho-renge-kyo and reveals the Law of Nam-myoho-renge-kyo inherent in one's life, one can manifest the life state of the Buddha of time without beginning. It means that ordinary people actually carry out the actions of that Buddha in their daily lives and society.

Soka Gakkai members pray to this Gohonzon as an embodiment, or mirror, of their innate Buddhahood—chanting Nam-myoho-renge-kyo with the conviction that they themselves are the Mystic

Law—and strive to teach and share this teaching with others. By doing so they will, just like Nichiren Daishonin, manifest the Mystic Law in their lives, revealing the state of Buddhahood and enjoying the benefit and good fortune that comes with it.

NOTES:

1. Saha world: *Saha* is a Sanskrit term that can be translated as "to endure." The saha world is one where people must endure ceaseless confusion and suffering, the real world in which we live at present.

2. In Kumarajiva's Chinese translation of the Lotus Sutra, the three powerful enemies are described in twenty lines in the "Encouraging Devotion" chapter's verse section.

3. The Ceremony in the Air: one of the assemblies described in the Lotus Sutra, in which the entire gathering is suspended in space above the ground. During the ceremony, Shakyamuni transfers the essence of the Lotus Sutra specifically to the Bodhisattvas of the Earth led by Superior Practices, entrusting them with its propagation in the Latter Day of the Law. The heart of the ceremony consists of the revelation of Shakyamuni's original enlightenment and the transfer of the essence of the sutra to the Bodhisattvas of the Earth.

CHAPTER

14

Three Thousand Realms in a Single Moment of Life

"**Three thousand realms** in a single moment of life" is a Buddhist teaching that reveals how ordinary people can attain Buddhahood. Studying this teaching deepens understanding of the way in which Nichiren Buddhism makes it possible for all people to attain enlightenment.

Three Thousand Realms in a Single Moment of Life

One of the philosophical principles forming the basis underlying Nichiren Daishonin's inscription of the Gohonzon of Nam-myoho-renge-kyo—the object of devotion for enabling all people of the Latter Day of the Law to attain Buddhahood—is the doctrine of three thousand realms in a single moment of life.

This was formulated by Great Teacher T'ien-t'ai (Zhiyi) of China in his work *Great Concentration and Insight* in order to help people put into practice the Lotus Sutra's teaching that all people can attain Buddhahood.

"A single moment of life" indicates one's life as it exists at any given moment. "Three thousand realms" refers to all phenomena—all things and their varied functions. The principle of three thousand realms in a single moment of life teaches that a single moment of life includes three thousand realms, and life at each moment permeates and pervades all of them.

Life at each moment contains limitless potential. When one transforms the state of one's life at this moment, the environment that surrounds it also changes, which can even result in a change in the entire world. Thus, the doctrine of three thousand realms in a single moment of life is a teaching of hope and transformation. Ikeda Sensei expresses the significance of this principle in describing the theme of his novel *The Human Revolution*:

> A great human revolution in just a single individual will help achieve a change in the destiny of a nation and, further, will enable a change in the destiny of all humankind.

In his work "The Object of Devotion for Observing the Mind," Nichiren Daishonin quotes a passage from T'ien-t'ai's *Great Concentration and Insight* that describes the three thousand realms in a single moment of life:

> Life at each moment is endowed with the Ten Worlds. At the same time, each of the Ten Worlds is endowed with all Ten Worlds, so that an entity of life actually possesses one hundred worlds. Each of these worlds in turn possesses thirty realms, which means that in the one hundred worlds there are three thousand realms. The three thousand realms of existence are all possessed by life in a single moment. If there is no life, that is the end of the matter. But if there is the slightest bit of life, it contains all the three thousand realms. (WND-1, 354)

In other words, so long as one is alive, one's life at each moment possesses three thousand realms, each of which is unique and distinct from the others.

The number three thousand comes from multiplying the mutual possession of the Ten Worlds (10 worlds × 10 worlds = 100 worlds) by the ten factors of life and then by the three realms of existence (100 × 10 × 3 = 3,000). The Ten Worlds, the ten factors, and the three realms are concepts that each approach life and the law of causality operating within it from a different perspective. Three thousand realms in a single moment of life incorporates all of these perspectives and thereby offers an encompassing view of one's life and the world as a whole.

The Mutual Possession of the Ten Worlds

The core principle underlying three thousand realms in a single moment of life is the mutual possession of the Ten Worlds. The Daishonin writes: "The doctrine of three thousand realms in a single moment of life begins with the concept of the mutual possession of the Ten Worlds" ("The Opening of the Eyes," WND-1, 224) and "[The Buddha] also expounded the doctrine of three thousand realms in a single moment of life, explaining that the nine worlds have the potential for Buddhahood and that Buddhahood retains the nine worlds" ("The Selection of the Time," WND-1, 539).

The Ten Worlds represent ten states of life. They are the worlds of (1) hell, (2) hungry spirits (hunger), (3) animals (animality), (4) asuras, (5) human beings (humanity), (6) heavenly beings (heaven), (7) voice-hearers (learning), (8) cause-awakened ones (realization), (9) bodhisattvas, and (10) Buddhas.

The sutras other than the Lotus Sutra teach that each of the Ten Worlds is a distinct and separate realm, or a fixed condition of life, and that one cannot move from any one of the Ten Worlds to another until after one dies, at which time one can be reborn into another of the Ten Worlds.

But the Lotus Sutra fundamentally overturns this idea, revealing that all people in any of the nine worlds other than Buddhahood also possess the world of Buddhahood. Conversely, the world of Buddhahood is endowed with all the other nine worlds.

The mutual possession of the Ten Worlds means that a life now manifesting any one of the Ten Worlds possesses all of the Ten Worlds. In that sense, Buddhas and all people of the nine worlds are equally endowed with all the Ten Worlds and are therefore essentially equal.

Also, if one's life is displaying a particular one of the Ten Worlds at this moment, it has the potential to manifest, in response to a condition or influence, another of the Ten Worlds at the next moment. It follows that anyone in any of the Ten Worlds, in response to the right conditions, can manifest the world of Buddhahood and become a Buddha.

The principle of the mutual possession of the Ten Worlds, then, explains that one can elevate one's state of life to that of bodhisattvas and even to Buddhahood in the course of this lifetime.

The Ten Factors of Life

There are ten aspects, or factors, common to all life in any of the Ten Worlds. From the world of hell to the world of Buddhahood, all lives in any of the Ten Worlds equally possess the ten factors of life. These ten factors describe the law of causality at work behind the changes in one's state of life.

The section of "Expedient Means," the second chapter of the Lotus Sutra, that Soka Gakkai members recite every day during the practice of gongyo describes the "true aspect of all phenomena" as follows:

> The true aspect of all phenomena can only be understood and shared between Buddhas. This reality consists of the appearance, nature, entity, power, influence, internal cause, relation, latent effect, manifest effect, and their consistency from beginning to end. (LSOC, 57)

To help people conceptualize the true aspect of all phenomena, the sutra introduces ten attributes, or factors. Each factor is prefaced by a term, pronounced *nyoze* in Japanese, meaning "like this," "such," or "thus."

Among the ten factors, "appearance" is the outward form or aspect of a living being that is subject to change from moment to moment.

"Nature" is the innate and consistent character or intrinsic attributes.

"Entity" is the thing or being itself, which has the aspects of appearance and nature.

The first three factors, appearance, nature, and entity, constitute the existence and essence of the living being. The remaining seven factors, in contrast, express the workings or functions of that life.

"Power" means internal energy or inner potential.

"Influence" is the outward expression of internal power and the influence of that power on other life or phenomena.

The next four factors, "internal cause," "relation," "latent effect," and "manifest effect," express the law of causality that governs the workings of life.

Internal cause is a primary or direct cause inherent in life that produces an effect or result.

Relation refers to an external condition or influence that stimulates the internal cause, functioning as a supporting or auxiliary cause to bring about an effect.

Latent effect is the intrinsic, imperceptible result arising from the interaction of the internal cause and the relation, or external cause.

Manifest effect is the evident result that emerges from the latent effect in response to the time and to external causes or conditions.

Finally, "consistency from beginning to end" means that all the other factors are consistent from the beginning—the first factor, appearance—to the end—the ninth factor, manifest effect. For example, a life presently in the world of Buddhahood will have the

10 Factors

Patterns of existence common to all phenomena in any of the Ten Worlds

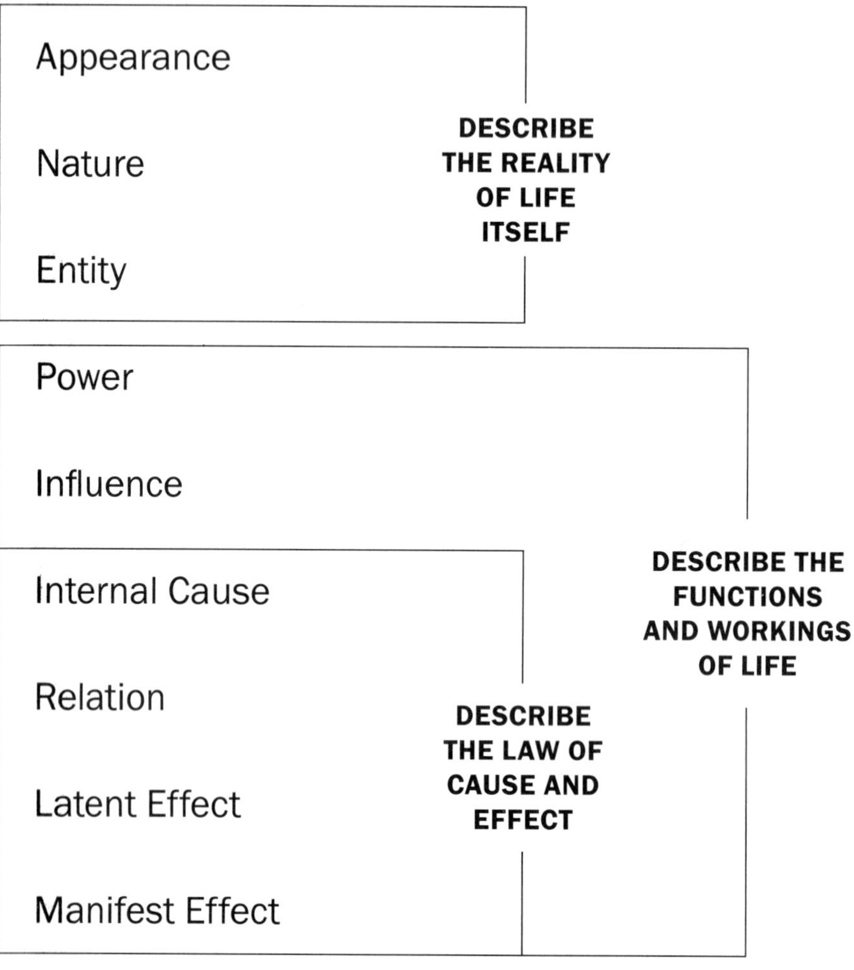

Consistency From Beginning to the End

appearance of Buddhahood, the nature of Buddhahood, all the way through the manifest effect of Buddhahood, and the same principle applies to each of the Ten Worlds.

Life in any of the Ten Worlds is equally endowed with the ten factors, that is, with the law of causality that governs changes in one's state of life. One's life, while displaying a particular one of the Ten Worlds, has the potential to manifest, in response to a condition or influence, any other of the Ten Worlds. It follows, then, that anyone in any of the Ten Worlds can, in response to the right conditions, manifest the world of Buddhahood and become a Buddha.

The Three Realms of Existence

The "three realms of existence" are "the realm of the five components," "the realm of living beings," and "the realm of the environment." Each of the Ten Worlds distinctly expresses itself in these three realms.

Living beings are classified according to their states of life, that is, the Ten Worlds, from moment to moment. The realm of living beings reflects the differences between these life states.

Buddhism regards a living being as a temporary union of five components. As such, living beings have no fixed or permanent existence of their own but are in a constant state of flux and change.

It is natural, therefore, that changes or distinctions in the life state of living beings, that is, in which of the Ten Worlds they manifest, are also evident in the five components that make up those living beings.

The five components are form, perception, conception, volition, and consciousness.

Form is the physical aspect of life, the body and its physical attributes.

Perception is the function of receiving and sensing information from and about the outside world through the six sense organs (eyes, ears, nose, tongue, body, and mind).

Conception is the function of forming impressions or ideas about what has been perceived.

Volition is what links the conception of what is perceived to action. It accords with the various workings of the heart and mind, such as will, wants, and desires.

Finally, consciousness describes the discerning function of life that recognizes and distinguishes things.

In the world of hell, the five components of life have characteristics specific to the world of hell, while in the world of Buddhahood they have characteristics specific to the world of Buddhahood. Thus the realm of the five components manifests the Ten Worlds.

The differences in the life state of living beings, or which of the Ten Worlds they manifest, are also manifest in the land or environment those beings inhabit, that is, the realm of the environment.

From the principle of the three realms of existence, we can see that when the state of the five components changes, that of living beings and their environments also changes. A change in the state of one's heart and mind will effect a change in every aspect of one's own life and one's environment.

The principles of the mutual possession of the Ten Worlds, the ten factors of life, and the three realms of existence, when merged together, form the three thousand realms in a single moment of life. This teaching provides a comprehensive view of the law of causality permeating life and the surrounding world and clarifies that all people are equally capable of attaining Buddhahood.

CHAPTER

15

Embracing the Gohonzon Is in Itself Observing One's Own Mind

The purpose of Buddhist practice is to establish, in this lifetime, the state of a Buddha, a life condition of absolute happiness unaffected by changes in one's circumstances or surroundings. It was for this purpose that Nichiren Daishonin inscribed the Gohonzon, or object of devotion, thereby establishing the way for everyone to open and reveal within their own lives the world of Buddhahood, to win in their daily affairs and to become victors in life.

This section will explain the significance of the Gohonzon and the principle that embracing the Gohonzon is in itself observing one's own mind, which makes it possible for all people to attain Buddhahood.

The Significance of the Gohonzon

An object of devotion or worship is that which is revered most highly in any religious tradition. In Buddhism, the object of devotion is most often a statue or image of a Buddha or bodhisattva. What a religious faith regards as its object of devotion indicates what is fundamental to its beliefs. It is the core element that determines how people embrace and carry out their faith in that religion.

The object of devotion fundamental to the faith of Soka Gakkai members is the Gohonzon of Nam-myoho-renge-kyo, which was established by Nichiren Daishonin.

The Seed of Buddhahood

Shakyamuni awakened to the fundamental Law that permeates all life and the universe, and for this reason he was called Buddha, or awakened one. He made it clear that all Buddhas attain enlightenment by awakening to this fundamental Law, the Mystic Law. Nam-myoho-renge-kyo is the Law that enables all people to attain Buddhahood, and it is also the name of that Law. In other words, Nichiren Daishonin taught and directly expressed the Law that constitutes the fundamental cause for attaining enlightenment as Nam-myoho-renge-kyo.

The Mystic Law, which is the cause, or seed, of Buddhahood, is essentially inherent in the lives of all living beings. This innate cause is also known as the Buddha nature, or the world of Buddhahood.

In this regard, the Daishonin states:

> When we revere Myoho-renge-kyo inherent in our own life as the object of devotion, the Buddha nature within us is summoned forth and manifested by our chanting of Nam-myoho-renge-kyo. This is what is meant by "Buddha." To illustrate, when a caged bird sings, birds who are flying in the sky are thereby summoned and gather around, and when the birds flying in the sky gather around, the bird in the cage strives to get out. When with our mouths we chant the Mystic Law, our Buddha nature, being summoned, will invariably emerge. The Buddha nature of Brahma and Shakra, being called, will protect us, and the Buddha nature of the Buddhas and bodhisattvas, being summoned, will rejoice. ("How Those Initially Aspiring to the Way Can Attain Buddhahood through the Lotus Sutra," WND-1, 887)

Nam-myoho-renge-kyo is the name of the world of Buddhahood inherent in one's own life and in all things. When one believes in the Gohonzon and chants Nam-myoho-renge-kyo, one awakens and summons the world of Buddhahood within one's life; and further, one calls forth the world of Buddhahood from within all things in the universe. In other words, one opens up the limitless potential of one's own life and activates the functions of the Buddhas, bodhisattvas, and heavenly beings—that is, the protective forces in one's environment.

"I, Nichiren, Have Inscribed My Life"

Nam-myoho-renge-kyo is the teaching hidden in the depths of the Lotus Sutra, which teaches that all people are capable of becoming Buddhas. Nichiren Daishonin awakened to the Mystic Law within his own life, realizing that it is synonymous with the world of Buddhahood. This Law, he said, is none other than Nam-myoho-renge-kyo, and he taught and spread it widely. He then expressed it in the Gohonzon as a focus for Buddhist practice.

The Daishonin says:

> I, Nichiren, have inscribed my life in sumi ink, so believe in the Gohonzon with your whole heart. The Buddha's will is the Lotus Sutra, but the soul of Nichiren is nothing other than Nam-myoho-renge-kyo. ("Reply to Kyo'o," WND-1, 412)

The Gohonzon is an expression of the world of Buddhahood in Nichiren Daishonin's life—the fundamental Law of Nam-myoho-renge-kyo that he awoke to, revealed, and embodied.

Down the center of the Gohonzon are inscribed the words "Nam-myoho-renge-kyo Nichiren." Nam-myoho-renge-kyo is the fundamental Law for attaining enlightenment, and Nichiren Daishonin, who revealed and taught the Law for all people, is none other than the Buddha of the Latter Day of the Law.

The Clear Mirror That Reflects One's Life

As an ordinary person, Nichiren Daishonin opened and revealed within his life the world of Buddhahood (Nam-myoho-renge-kyo). This is the most ideal state of life, which all people can aspire to attain. Therefore, the Daishonin expressed it in the form of a mandala as the object of devotion, establishing the way for ordinary people to make their innate world of Buddhahood the foundation of their being. When they believe in and pray to the Gohonzon, they can immediately observe the world of Buddhahood inherent in their lives, just as the Daishonin did.

Nichiren Daishonin delved deeply into the Lotus Sutra, which teaches that all people are endowed with the world of Buddhahood, and found in its depths the fundamental Law for attaining Buddhahood. He revealed that Law directly as Nam-myoho-renge-kyo and established the Gohonzon as its concrete expression in order to assist people in their practice for attaining Buddhahood. The Gohonzon, in this sense, can be viewed as a clear mirror that reflects the world of Buddhahood within ordinary people and allows them to observe it and bring it forth.

The Ceremony in the Air

Nichiren Daishonin inscribed the Gohonzon as a mandala depicting in written characters the Ceremony in the Air described in the Lotus Sutra. The ceremony begins in "The Emergence of the Treasure Tower," the eleventh chapter of the sutra, with the appearance of the treasure tower of the Buddha named Many Treasures and the entire assembly being suspended in the air. It ends in "Entrustment," the twenty-second chapter, with the closing of the doors of the treasure tower.

The core elements of this ceremony are as follows: Shakyamuni, having revealed his true identity as the eternal Buddha, entrusts to the Bodhisattvas of the Earth, his eternal disciples whom he has summoned from beneath the earth, the task of spreading the Lotus Sutra in the evil age after his passing in order to save the people of that age from suffering and lead them to happiness.

These events occur over eight chapters, beginning with "Emerging from the Earth," the fifteenth chapter, and continuing through the "Entrustment" chapter. The Daishonin inscribed the Gohonzon based on the description of this ceremony of entrustment in the Lotus Sutra.

A key element for attaining Buddhahood taught in the Lotus Sutra is to make people aware that the world of Buddhahood is inherent in their own lives and to enable them to unlock and bring forth that world of Buddhahood from within. The Daishonin made use of the motif of the treasure tower, which is central to the Lotus Sutra's Ceremony in the Air, in creating the image of the Gohonzon. He depicted the treasure tower as Nam-myoho-renge-kyo, which he inscribed down the center of the Gohonzon. He states, "In the Latter Day of the Law, no treasure tower exists other than the figures of the men and women who embrace the Lotus Sutra" ("On the Treasure Tower," WND-1, 299), clarifying that the treasure tower represents the very life of all those who believe in the Mystic Law.

The Daishonin teaches that Shakyamuni and Many Treasures, as they appear in the Ceremony in the Air, represent the world of Buddhahood inherent in all living beings and that the Bodhisattvas of the Earth, led by Bodhisattva Superior Practices and others, indicate the world of bodhisattvas also innate within all people. Assembled at the Ceremony in the Air are voice-hearers, heavenly gods and benevolent deities, and other living beings. Representatives from among these various beings of each of the Ten Worlds are included on the Gohonzon.

The Daishonin expressed his enlightenment in the Gohonzon, which he called a *mandala*. This Sanskrit word refers to a depiction of the Buddha and those who have gathered to hear him preach and is also interpreted as meaning "perfectly endowed" and "cluster of blessings." This Gohonzon of Nam-myoho-renge-kyo is perfectly endowed because it includes all of the Ten Worlds. It is a cluster of blessings because it possesses all the wonderful attributes of the Ten Worlds. In essence, the Gohonzon is the mandala that is fully endowed with the Ten Worlds.

The Gohonzon represents the life state of the Buddha, which is Nam-myoho-renge-kyo itself, eternally endowed with all of the Ten Worlds, as well as the superior attributes inherent in each of these worlds. When people believe in this Gohonzon and base their lives on it, aware that they themselves are Nam-myoho-renge-kyo, they can freely and fully display the dignified, unique attributes of each of the Ten Worlds inherent in their lives.

The Actual Three Thousand Realms in a Single Moment of Life

The Gohonzon, which is fully endowed with the Ten Worlds, expresses the principle of their mutual possession—that life in any of the Ten Worlds is endowed with all the Ten Worlds. This means that a living being in any of the Ten Worlds can, through encountering the right condition or influence, manifest the world of Buddhahood and become a Buddha.

The mutual possession of the Ten Worlds is core to the doctrine of three thousand realms in a single moment of life, which crystallizes and explains, for the purpose of putting it into practice, the philosophy that all people are capable of attaining Buddhahood.

The doctrine of three thousand realms in a single moment of life is described by Great Teacher T'ien-t'ai (Zhiyi) in his work *Great Concentration and Insight*. It explains that all people innately possess the essential cause for attaining enlightenment and makes it conceptually clear that all people have the potential to become Buddhas. But while T'ien-t'ai refers to this doctrine as the three thousand realms in a single moment of life, it is at this point still in the realm of theory.

In contrast, Nichiren Daishonin, through his wisdom, perceived the fundamental Law of enlightenment that is Nam-myoho-renge-kyo. And, out of his compassionate desire to save all people, he endured countless obstacles and hardships, exhibiting the behavior of a Buddha as an ordinary human being.

The Gohonzon, in which the Daishonin directly revealed his life state of Buddhahood—a state he had brought forth from within as an ordinary person—is a concrete expression of the principle of three thousand realms in a single moment of life. The Gohonzon is therefore referred to as the "actual" three thousand realms in a single moment of life.

Nichiren Daishonin called the Gohonzon the "banner of propagation of the Lotus Sutra" ("The Real Aspect of the Gohonzon," WND-1, 831). In the Ceremony in the Air, Shakyamuni entrusts the Bodhisattvas of the Earth with the mission of spreading the Mystic Law in the evil age after his passing. The Gohonzon exemplifies this intent of the Buddha. To spread faith in the Gohonzon is to spread the Lotus Sutra, opening the way for kosen-rufu, the widespread propagation of the Mystic Law.

Embracing the Gohonzon Is in Itself Observing One's Own Mind

The Lotus Sutra makes clear that all people innately possess the wisdom and compassion of a Buddha. It teaches that the ultimate purpose of a Buddha's appearance in this world is to open up this Buddha wisdom in all living beings.

Meditation, a central element of Buddhist practice, means to focus one's mind on cultivating and bringing forth wisdom. In particular, it means to observe one's own life, or mind, based upon the principles taught in the Buddhist scriptures. "Observing the mind" is a practice carried out in order to attain Buddhahood.

By deeply observing the workings of his own mind, T'ien-t'ai came to realize that his life possessed all of the Ten Worlds, and in this way he understood the principle of the mutual possession of the Ten Worlds. He taught the practice of observing the mind as the means for awakening to the reality that life at each moment is endowed with three thousand realms, or all phenomena. This is the doctrine of three thousand realms in a single moment of life.

To prepare people for the practice of observing the mind, T'ien-t'ai formulated a variety of disciplines for leading people through graduated levels of development, or awakening. But these were in reality extremely difficult, requiring superior capacity and intensive effort. Those who arrived at a genuine awakening through such methods were very few indeed.

In contrast to T'ien-t'ai and his approach, Nichiren Daishonin studied and searched for a way of Buddhist practice that would be accessible to everyone and make it possible for anyone to attain Buddhahood. This search culminated in his teaching the practice of chanting Nam-myoho-renge-kyo with faith in the Gohonzon as the way for all people to achieve genuine happiness.

Nam-myoho-renge-kyo is the fundamental Law to which all Buddhas awaken when they attain enlightenment, and it is the basis for the various workings of the life states of the Ten Worlds. The Gohonzon of Nam-myoho-renge-kyo reveals the true nature of the lives of all people as being fully endowed with the Ten Worlds.

Those who believe in and pray to the Gohonzon are able to observe the Ten Worlds operating within their own lives. Prior to the Daishonin revealing his teaching, the practice for attaining Buddhahood was based on observation of the mind. But in Nichiren Buddhism, it is accomplished through faith in and practice to the Gohonzon. This is the teaching that embracing the Gohonzon is in itself observing one's own mind.

In "The Object of Devotion for Observing the Mind" the Daishonin states:

> Shakyamuni's practices and the virtues he consequently attained are all contained within the five characters of Myoho-renge-kyo. If we believe in these five characters, we will naturally be granted the same benefits as he was. (WND-1, 365)

All of the vast number of practices (causes) that Shakyamuni carried out and that enabled him to attain Buddhahood and the benefits and virtues (effects) he attained as a result of those practices are encompassed within the seed of Buddhahood, the five characters of Myoho-renge-kyo, that is, in Nam-myoho-renge-kyo.

Having expressed Nam-myoho-renge-kyo in the form of a mandala that is the Gohonzon, or object of devotion for Buddhist practice, the Daishonin is saying in the above passage that when ordinary people of the Latter Day of the Law embrace this Gohonzon, they will be able to obtain for themselves the benefits of all the causes and effects of all the practices carried out by the Buddha.

CHAPTER

16

The Mission and Practice of the Bodhisattvas of the Earth

This chapter will explain the fundamental spirit and attitude of faith in light of the mission and practice of the Bodhisattvas of the Earth, who aim to accomplish kosen-rufu.

The Mission and Awareness of the Bodhisattvas of the Earth

The Bodhisattvas of the Earth are the disciples whom the eternal Buddha had personally instructed and trained.

What is the abiding wish of Shakyamuni, who was revealed to be the eternal Buddha in the Lotus Sutra? That wish is expressed as follows at the end of "Life Span," the sixteenth chapter:

> At all times I [Shakyamuni] think to myself: How can I cause living beings to gain entry into the unsurpassed way and quickly acquire the body of a Buddha? (LSOC, 273).

Nichiren Daishonin refers to this wish in his writings as the compassionate desire of the Buddha.

The Vow of the Bodhisattvas of the Earth and the Buddha's Entrustment of His Teachings

In "Emerging from the Earth," the fifteenth chapter of the sutra, Shakyamuni urges his disciples to spread the Lotus Sutra in the evil age after his passing, and then he summons forth from beneath the earth those who are qualified to be entrusted with this task. They are known as the Bodhisattvas of the Earth.

In "Supernatural Powers," the twenty-first chapter, the Bodhisattvas of the Earth, responding to Shakyamuni's appeal to propagate the sutra in that age, make a vow to teach and spread among the people the fundamental Law for attaining Buddhahood. They take to heart, inherit as their own, and strive to actualize the great desire of their teacher, the eternal Buddha. This desire shared by mentor and disciples is to achieve kosen-rufu, the widespread propagation of the Lotus Sutra's teachings. Accepting their pledge, Shakyamuni entrusts to them the future propagation of the Mystic Law.

Had the Bodhisattvas of the Earth not made their appearance, the compassionate desire of the Buddha would not be realized. One person takes a stand with an awareness as a Bodhisattva of the Earth, aims to build a world where people can live in peace and happiness based on the Mystic Law, and enables two, three, and eventually countless people to awaken as well. These individuals will then encourage one another to fully display their distinctive qualities and abilities and will work together actively to achieve these goals. Kosen-rufu is realized through the existence of such an active alliance of unique individuals.

Where there are the powers of faith and practice of the Bodhisattvas of the Earth who persist in fulfilling the vow for kosen-rufu, the boundless powers of the Buddha and the Law inherent in the Mystic Law will clearly emerge, making it possible to transform the suffering-filled saha world into the Land of Eternally Tranquil Light, in which the life force of Buddhahood is always present.

When the life force deriving from that great vow pervades all three thousand realms of phenomena—the entire universe—a society of great well-being that is embraced in the compassion and wisdom of the Buddha will emerge.

Ikeda Sensei states:

> The heart of the great vow for kosen-rufu and the life state of Buddhahood are one and the same. Therefore, when we dedicate our lives to this vow, we can bring forth the supreme nobility, strength, and greatness of our lives. When we remain true to this vow, the limitless courage, wisdom, and compassion of the Buddha flow forth from within us. When we wholeheartedly strive to realize this vow, the "poison" of even the most difficult challenge can be transformed into "medicine," and karma transformed into mission.[1]

The Great Vow to Propagate the Lotus Sutra

Nichiren Daishonin states, "The 'great vow' refers to the propagation of the Lotus Sutra" (OTT, 82). The Lotus Sutra teaches that the lives of all people are endowed with the supremely noble Buddha nature. In it, the mission of spreading the Mystic Law, which enables all people to attain Buddhahood, throughout Jambudvipa—the entire world—is entrusted to the Bodhisattvas of the Earth. The Daishonin dedicated his life to the goal of fulfilling this great vow of propagating the Lotus Sutra, the vow to accomplish kosen-rufu.

The Daishonin awakened to this Law within his own life—the Law of Nam-myoho-renge-kyo, which is the essence of the Lotus Sutra—and he made a great vow to spread it widely. He pledged to become the "pillar," the "eyes," and the "great ship" that could protect, support, teach, and guide all people, stating, "This is my vow, and I will never forsake it!" (WND-1, 281). Unperturbed and unbowed by any number of great difficulties, he kept his promise never to retreat in this endeavor while maintaining a noble state of life capable of liberating the people from suffering.

Urging his followers to take up the same task, the Daishonin told them, "My wish is that all my disciples make a great vow" ("The Dragon Gate," WND-1, 1003), and entrusted them with the mission of achieving kosen-rufu.

The Soka Gakkai Is Advancing in Accord With the Buddha's Intent

The Soka Gakkai has emerged in modern times in accord with the Buddha's intent and has taken responsibility to fulfill the vow for kosen-rufu, succeeding to the will of Nichiren Daishonin. It reveres the Gohonzon, which the Daishonin described as "the banner of propagation of the Lotus Sutra" ("The Real Aspect of the Gohonzon," WND-1, 831), and its members have been exerting themselves in the compassionate practice of spreading faith in it, thereby achieving unprecedented development in the worldwide movement for kosen-rufu. Convinced of this noble mission, second Soka Gakkai president Josei Toda declared that the organization's name would be recorded in Buddhist scriptures of the future as "Soka Gakkai Buddha."

The great vow of Nichiren Daishonin is nothing other than kosen-rufu. This is also the great vow of the mentors and disciples of the Soka Gakkai—the three founding presidents—and the members throughout the world who have fought along with them. They have stood up together with a deep awareness as the Daishonin's direct disciples and a burning sense of mission as the Bodhisattvas of the Earth.

Sensei writes:

> Dedicated to the mission of spreading the Mystic Law and realizing kosen-rufu through compassionate propagation, Soka Gakkai members are all Bodhisattvas of the Earth. They are emissaries of the Buddha. When they take action with that awareness, they

> undergo a profound inner transformation, and the powerful life force to triumph over any storm of karma flows within them.[2]

How can the Bodhisattvas of the Earth be described in today's world? They are people who live to fulfill the mission of transmitting the fundamental Law for attaining Buddhahood in the midst of the most troubled times and social circumstances, allowing those burdened with the greatest misery and hardship to tap the power to build genuine happiness. With the conviction that those who suffer the most have the right to enjoy the greatest happiness, they go to the side of suffering people, teach them the Mystic Law, and together with them walk the path to transforming their destiny. People who act in this way are the Bodhisattvas of the Earth.

Perceiving Evil and Protecting Good

Good Friends in the Realm of Buddhism

In Buddhism, the terms *good friend* and *evil friend* are used to indicate persons who have some influence, either good or bad, on one's thinking and Buddhist practice.

Good friends are those who lead one to the correct teaching or help one practice toward enlightenment. They can include Buddhist teachers and fellow practitioners. Evil friends are those who interfere with or obstruct one's Buddhist practice, leading one away from enlightenment and toward the evil paths, or suffering. It is important to be close to good friends and to wisely take care not to be deceived or influenced by evil friends.

The human mind can easily be swayed or shaken. In carrying out Buddhist practice, there is a possibility of giving in to one's weaknesses and failing to apply oneself, thereby losing sight of the Buddha's correct teaching. That is why it is essential to have good friends who can inspire one's faith and always direct one on the correct path to Buddhahood. Nichiren Daishonin writes:

> Therefore, the best way to attain Buddhahood is to encounter a good friend. How far can our own wisdom take us? If we have even enough wisdom to distinguish hot from cold, we should seek out a good friend. ("Three Tripitaka Masters Pray for Rain," WND-1, 598)

With regard to evil friends who can obstruct one's Buddhist practice, the Daishonin quotes the Nirvana Sutra:

> Have no fear of mad elephants. What you should fear are evil friends! Why? Because a mad elephant can only destroy your body; it cannot destroy your mind. But an evil friend can destroy both body and mind. . . . Even if you are killed by a mad elephant, you will not fall into the three evil paths [the realms of hell, hungry spirits, and animals]. But if you are killed by an evil friend, you are certain to fall into them. ("On Reciting the Daimoku of the Lotus Sutra," WND-2, 220)

Faith for Transforming Evil Friends Into Good Friends

Not only did the Daishonin teach that one should not follow or be influenced by evil friends, he also taught that one should establish faith strong enough to defeat their attempts to impede one's Buddhist practice and regard them as opportunities to further advance toward one's attainment of Buddhahood.

The stronger one's faith and practice becomes, the more strongly the three obstacles and four devils and the three powerful enemies will emerge to interfere. If, however, through summoning even stronger faith and using the wisdom gained from the Daishonin's writings, one can clearly perceive devilish functions for what they are, they will at that point cease to function as devils.

Through challenging and overcoming such obstacles based on faith in the Gohonzon, one will be able to bring forth from within previously untapped power and tremendous potential, strengthen one's faith, and further develop one's state of life. In other words, one can transform evil friends into good friends.

In "The Actions of the Votary of the Lotus Sutra," the Daishonin writes: "Devadatta was the foremost good friend to Thus Come One Shakyamuni. In this age as well, it is not one's allies but one's powerful enemies who assist one's progress" (WND-1, 770), and in the letter titled "Why No Protection from the Heavenly Gods?" he states, "Evil persons too will be good friends to me" (WND-2, 432).

Strictness Toward Slander and Flexibility Toward Culture and Customs

Strictly Admonishing Slander of the Law

"Slander of the Law" means maligning, defaming, or speaking ill of the correct Buddhist teaching. The correct teaching means the truth to which the Buddha awakened, the teaching that enables all people to attain Buddhahood. It was expounded by Shakyamuni in the Lotus Sutra, the essence of which Nichiren Daishonin revealed to be Nam-myoho-renge-kyo.

This correct teaching represents a view of life and the human being that regards everyone's life as innately possessing the noble state of Buddhahood and being replete with unlimited potential. To oppose and disparage this correct teaching or to reject it and refuse to believe in it constitutes slander of the Law.

Such slander is an expression of disbelief in and opposition to the most humane and genuine way of life that aims for the happiness of self and others and a peaceful and tranquil society; it is the root cause of unhappiness and should therefore be strictly admonished.

That said, however, one should not reject or exclude people who don't recognize or support one's faith, nor should one try to force one's beliefs on others.

During the Daishonin's lifetime, the various Buddhist schools spread erroneous doctrines that disparaged the Lotus Sutra, and slander of the Law became widespread. In his treatise "On Establishing the Correct Teaching for the Peace of the Land," the Daishonin defines slander of the Law as the one evil that is the source of both people's suffering and the instability of society. He strongly advocates building, through faith in the correct teaching, a peaceful society in which people can feel at ease.

In order to attain Buddhahood, it is not enough to simply refrain from committing slander oneself. It is also important to strictly admonish and challenge the slander of others, endeavor to correct them, and free them from the path to suffering. This is the compassionate practice of shakubuku, spreading the teachings while challenging and defeating slander.

The Daishonin teaches, "To hope to attain Buddhahood without speaking out against slander is as futile as trying to find water in the midst of fire or fire in the midst of water" ("The Essentials for Attaining Buddhahood," WND-1, 747).

To challenge evil influences that spread slander of the Law serves to empower and increase the virtuous forces of the Buddha and to protect oneself from evil, making the attainment of Buddhahood possible.

The Precept of Adapting to Local Customs

Buddhism teaches the fundamental principle for living a full and satisfying life. It is a principle accessible to all people regardless of the time or country in which they live, their ethnicity, gender identity, or age. As the Lotus Sutra teaches, all human beings, regardless of how they may differ, have the potential to attain Buddhahood, and this is why Nichiren Buddhism in particular recognizes and affords utmost respect to cultural diversity.

The Daishonin refers to a Buddhist principle called the "precept of adapting to local customs," which teaches that one should respect and abide by the culture and traditions of each country and region, as well as by the customs of the times, to the extent that they do not violate the fundamental teachings of Buddhism.

He writes:

> The meaning of this precept is that, so long as no seriously offensive act is involved, then even if one were to depart to some slight degree from the teachings of Buddhism, it would be better to avoid going against the manners and customs of the country. This is a precept expounded by the Buddha. ("The Recitation of the 'Expedient Means' and 'Life Span' Chapters," WND-1, 72)

Buddhism aims to uplift and enrich people's behavior, enabling them to lead a truly humane way of life. The customs and traditions of a society encompass the wisdom of its constituent communities and cultures. Much of that wisdom may accord with the teachings of Buddhism and surely include aspects of Buddhist wisdom. Manners, customs, and traditions that cultivate rich humanity become an entry point for introducing the wisdom of Buddhism.

On the other hand, when introducing the teachings of Buddhism from one culture or society to another, one must take care not to be overly attached to superficial aspects of either culture or inflexible about inessential elements of tradition or formality to the degree that one overlooks the fundamental spirit of Buddhism. To do so would be to confuse the insignificant with the essential and meaningful and would constitute a serious error. What is essential is to establish a peaceful and prosperous society through one's unwavering faith and practice while advancing one's human revolution and making significant contributions to one's community.

NOTES:

1. Daisaku Ikeda, "The Great Vow for the Happiness of All Humanity," *Living Buddhism*, January 2014, 8.

2. Daisaku Ikeda, *The New Human Revolution*, vol. 27 (Santa Monica, CA: World Tribune Press, 2022), 160.

CHAPTER

17

The Lineage and Tradition of Buddhist Humanism

The Soka Gakkai is a religious organization that practices Buddhist teachings originating from Shakyamuni Buddha in India and carried on and developed by the Indian Buddhist scholars Nagarjuna and Vasubandhu, who were revered as bodhisattvas; Great Teachers T'ien-t'ai (Zhiyi) and Miao-lo (Zhanran) of China; Great Teacher Dengyo (Saicho) of Japan; and Nichiren Daishonin. It maintains the orthodox lineage and tradition of Buddhist humanism that began with Shakyamuni, which affirms respect for life and for all human beings.

The Soka Gakkai bases itself on the Lotus Sutra, a central scripture of Mahayana Buddhism, and engages in Buddhist practice and activities adapted to modern times. It carries on the fundamental spirit of the Lotus Sutra as taught and exemplified by Nichiren Daishonin through his life and actions.

Shakyamuni

Shakyamuni was born a prince in ancient India. (His birthplace, Lumbini, is located in what is today Nepal.)

In his youth, Shakyamuni witnessed the unavoidable sufferings of existence—birth, aging, sickness, and death. Though still young and in good health, he realized that he, too, would someday experience them. He decided to leave his home and embark on a spiritual quest to find a solution to these fundamental sufferings.

As a prince, Shakyamuni led a life of great comfort and ease such that most people would envy. But when he became aware that the riches and luxuries people sought in life were ultimately fleeting and empty, he could find in them no real pleasure. This led him to search for a philosophy or teaching that would clarify the true meaning of human existence.

Buddha—The Awakened One

Shakyamuni was not satisfied with either the traditional spiritual teachings of India or the new schools of thought and belief that had become prevalent at that time. He sought instead through the practice of meditation to discover the fundamental causes and solutions to life's sufferings. In this way, he awakened to the eternal and universal Dharma, or Law, that pervades all life and the universe.

The name Shakyamuni is an honorific title meaning sage of the Shakyas—Shakya is the name of the clan to which he belonged and *muni* means sage. The title Buddha, by which he came to be universally known, means awakened one.

The Law to which Shakyamuni awakened became the core of the Buddhist teachings.

The Wisdom to Realize the Inherent Dignity of Life

Shakyamuni declared that people's ignorance of the inherent dignity of their own lives results in their being ruled by egoism. This causes them to be consumed by immediate, selfish desires and to be driven to seek their own happiness at the expense of others. He taught, therefore, that the noblest and most admirable way for people to live with true dignity is to awaken to the eternal and universal Law within them and return to their original pure state of life that is free of fundamental ignorance or darkness.

The Buddha's teaching in this regard amounted to what might be called a restoration of the value of the human being. It stressed how important it is for people to regain the supreme dignity of their lives and realize their infinite potential by bringing forth their inherent wisdom.

The Compassion to Respect All People

By awakening people to the value and dignity of their own lives, Shakyamuni taught them to understand and respect the value and dignity of others' lives as well. This is the basic spirit of Buddhist compassion.

Shakyamuni once explained to a certain king that all individuals hold themselves most dear and that therefore those who love themselves should not harm others.

Compassion as taught in Buddhism means to understand that others are as important and precious as we are and, as such, we should treasure them as we would treasure ourselves. It is a teaching of mutual understanding and respect.

The Lotus Sutra—The Essence of Mahayana Buddhism

Shakyamuni expounded his teachings for some fifty years, and after his death, his disciples compiled records of his words and actions. Those containing the Buddha's main doctrinal teachings came to be known as "sutras." Among all his teachings, those pertaining to compassion and wisdom are the focus of the Mahayana sutras. And preeminent among these is the Lotus Sutra, which has been extolled as the king of sutras.

In the Lotus Sutra, the Buddha says that by expounding it, he has fulfilled the wish he has held since the remote past to elevate all people to the same life state as his own. Further, he repeatedly calls upon countless disciples to inherit and share that eternal wish, or vow, and carry out the practice of compassion in order to fulfill it.

Nichiren Daishonin—The Votary of the Lotus Sutra

Nichiren Daishonin regarded the suffering of all people as his own and in a time of great social turmoil sought to find a way to relieve that suffering. He vowed to identify and carry on the Buddhist teachings capable of realizing genuine happiness for all people and establishing respect for human dignity. He studied the commentaries and writings of earlier Buddhist scholars while carefully reading and examining on his own the many Buddhist sutras. As a result of his studies, he found the answer he had been searching for in the Lotus Sutra, which teaches the way for all people to give expression to their unlimited potential and bring it to life in human society.

Based on these principles of the Lotus Sutra, the Daishonin strongly resolved to help all people realize true happiness and live with dignity and to actualize peace and security in society. He encountered life-threatening persecution by the authorities and fierce opposition from among the populace, owing to their lack of understanding of the correct teaching of Buddhism and their mistaken attachment to old ways of thinking. However, none of this deterred him in the least. He was a votary of the Lotus Sutra who took action in exact accord with the teachings of the sutra, encouraging and revitalizing the people even at the risk of his life.

Nichiren Daishonin established the practice of chanting Nam-myoho-renge-kyo, and he inscribed the Gohonzon as the object of faith, or devotion. By identifying, revealing, and establishing the teaching that is the essence of the Lotus Sutra, he opened the way for all people to attain Buddhahood.

In his treatise "On Establishing the Correct Teaching for the Peace of the Land," the Daishonin asserts that peace and social prosperity are indispensable to building individual happiness. He writes:

> If the nation is destroyed and people's homes are wiped out, then where can one flee for safety? If you care anything about your personal security, you should first of all pray for order and tranquillity throughout the four quarters of the land, should you not? (WND-1, 24)

The focus of the Daishonin's lifelong efforts was establishing the correct teaching for the peace of the land—that is, establishing the philosophy of respect for the dignity of life as society's guiding principle and building a world where people can live in peace and security.

This accords with efforts that practitioners of Buddhism have made since the time of Shakyamuni to overcome the destructive nature of egoism that inflicts so much harm and suffering on people and society. It marked a new humanistic approach based on the fundamental spirit of Buddhism to enable people to realize happiness for themselves and for others—one that sought to foster trust, value creation, and harmony.

Key to this process was dialogue grounded in reason and humanity.

The Soka Gakkai—Bringing Nichiren Buddhism to Life in Modern Times

Through their selfless efforts, the Soka Gakkai's three founding presidents—Tsunesaburo Makiguchi, Josei Toda, and Daisaku Ikeda—revived the philosophy and practice of Nichiren Daishonin in modern times.

Soka Gakkai members engage in a variety of activities based on the guidance of the three founding presidents.

On a personal level, while challenging themselves in all areas of life, they use the practice of chanting Nam-myoho-renge-kyo to reflect deeply on their lives and bring forth the hope and courage to deal with problems they encounter. In addition, they strive to develop rich character based on a solid commitment to humanistic values. This is the practice of human revolution.

Through everyday conversations with fellow members and attending Soka Gakkai meetings, members also deepen their understanding of Nichiren Daishonin's writings and Ikeda Sensei's guidance, share experiences in faith, and encourage and support one another.

In addition, they talk with friends and acquaintances about the principles and ideals of Buddhism and how their Buddhist practice has enriched their lives. In this way, they spread understanding and support for the life-affirming philosophy of Nichiren Buddhism and the humanistic activities of the Soka Gakkai while expanding the network of those who embrace faith in the Mystic Law.

The Westward Transmission of Buddhism and Worldwide Kosen-rufu

The practice of Nichiren Buddhism aims to enable people to realize happiness both for themselves and for others. It also places importance on individuals contributing to their communities as good citizens and becoming indispensable people whom others can trust and count on by fulfilling their roles at home, at work, and in society.

The Soka Gakkai is also actively engaged in addressing the global issues facing humanity today. Through its international antinuclear weapons exhibitions and initiatives in support of refugees, it highlights the importance of peace, respect for the dignity of life, and human rights. Also, through exhibitions on environmental themes, it aims to promote awareness of the need for efforts to protect the global environment.

The Soka Gakkai rediscovered the tradition of humanistic philosophy and practice originating with Shakyamuni and inherited by

Nichiren Daishonin, recognizing and treasuring it as the very essence of Buddhism. In addition, the Soka Gakkai is carrying on this tradition and spirit in today's society and through its activities and initiatives working to pass them on to future generations.

Through dialogue aimed at deepening understanding and providing inspiration, members of the Soka Gakkai strive continually to cultivate and empower many able individuals who can, in their respective roles and fields, exemplify Buddhist humanism. This movement, which aims to realize the happiness of humanity as well as world peace, is called kosen-rufu.

Buddhism, which began in India, traveled eastward to Japan. Now, it is being transmitted back westward, spreading not only to the countries of Asia and India but throughout the entire world. This is referred to as the westward transmission or westward return of Buddhism. Today, the Soka Gakkai's humanistic Buddhist movement has spread to 192 countries and territories around the globe.

The Three Treasures

The Soka Gakkai is the organization that in modern times has inherited the true spirit and lineage of Buddhism passed on from Shakyamuni.

It is a basic premise for all Buddhists to respect and treasure the Buddha, the Law (the Buddha's teachings), and the practitioners of the Law. Therefore, these three are regarded respectively as the treasure of the Buddha, the treasure of the Law, and the treasure of the Buddhist Order (community of believers). Together, they are known as the three treasures. The treasure of the Buddha is the Buddha who expounds the teaching, while the treasure of the Law is the teaching the Buddha expounds, and the treasure of the Buddhist Order is the gathering of people who believe in and practice that teaching.

In Sanskrit, the three treasures (*triratna*) are called Buddha,

Dharma, and Samgha. The word *samgha* originally meant a collective body or an assembly. Referring to the Buddhist Order, it was rendered phonetically into Chinese and then into Japanese with two characters, pronounced in Japanese as *sogya*. This was subsequently contracted to only the first character, *so*, which also came to be used to refer to Buddhist priests. Later, the term *samgha* was also rendered into Chinese and Japanese using two or three characters literally meaning a harmonious gathering, pronounced in Japanese as *wago* or *wago-so*.

Over the long history of Buddhism, various teachings emerged to guide people according to their needs and capacities, the times, and changes that took place in society.

The specific description of the three treasures differs somewhat within each teaching. In East Asia, the treasure of the Buddhist Order, or Samgha, came to refer exclusively to male Buddhist priests, not the community of believers as a whole.

In Nichiren Daishonin's Buddhism of sowing (that is, sowing the seeds of enlightenment, namely, Nam-myoho-renge-kyo), we revere the three treasures from the perspective of time without beginning, the fundamental dimension of existence. "Time without beginning" here is used to describe that which has always been present since the remotest past and will remain present into the eternal future. In terms of Buddhist practice, it refers to the original moment of attaining Buddhahood, when ordinary people reveal and manifest the eternal Mystic Law that has always been present within. Members of the Soka Gakkai eternally revere these three treasures in order to attain Buddhahood.

The treasure of the Buddha from the perspective of time without beginning is Nichiren Daishonin, the Buddha of beginningless time, or eternal Buddha, who revealed in his own life as an ordinary person the fundamental Law for attaining Buddhahood.

The treasure of the Law from the perspective of time without beginning is the Gohonzon, or object of devotion, of Nam-myoho-renge-kyo, which the Daishonin revealed as the Law for universal enlightenment.

The treasure of the Buddhist Order from the perspective of time without beginning is Nikko Shonin (the Daishonin's closest disciple and immediate successor), who protected and correctly transmitted the treasure of the Buddha and the treasure of the Law.

These are the three treasures to be revered in Nichiren Daishonin's Buddhism of sowing.[1]

When we revere (*nam*) these three treasures, we receive the benefit of sowing the seeds of enlightenment [Nam-myoho-renge-kyo] and are thereby able to attain Buddhahood.

The word *nam* derives from the Sanskrit word *namas* (meaning bow or reverence) and was translated into Chinese as "to devote one's life," meaning to base oneself on something and follow it in body and mind and to believe in it and make it one's foundation.

Moreover, the treasure of the Buddhist Order in a broad sense refers to the gathering of people who correctly protect, transmit, and spread the three treasures as objects of respect and reverence. Today, the Soka Gakkai is the treasure of the Buddhist Order, for it is the organization that is carrying on the spirit and conduct of Nichiren Daishonin and advancing worldwide kosen-rufu.

NOTE:

1. In Nichiren's Buddhism, the Buddhism of sowing indicates the teachings of Nichiren, in contrast with those of Shakyamuni, which are called the Buddhism of the harvest. The Buddhism of the harvest consists of teachings that can lead to enlightenment only those who received the seeds of Buddhahood by practicing Shakyamuni's teaching in previous lifetimes. In contrast, the Buddhism of sowing implants the seeds of Buddhahood, or Nam-myoho-renge-kyo, in the lives of those who had no connection with the Buddha's teaching in their past existences, i.e., the people of the Latter Day of the Law.

CHAPTER

18

Studying the Writings of Nichiren Daishonin

"On Establishing the Correct Teaching for the Peace of the Land": Engaging in Dialogues of Hope to Bring Happiness and Peace to All People

When we examine this wide variety of sutras, we find that they all stress how grave a matter it is to slander the correct teaching. How pitiful that people should all go out of the gate of the correct teaching and enter so deep into the prison of these distorted doctrines! How stupid that they should fall one after another into the snares of these evil doctrines and remain for so long entangled in this net of slanderous teachings! They lose their way in these mists and miasmas, and sink down amid the raging flames of hell. How could one not grieve? How could one not suffer?

Therefore, you must quickly reform the tenets that you hold in your heart and embrace the one true vehicle, the single good doctrine [of the Lotus Sutra]. If you do so, then the threefold world will become the Buddha land, and how could a Buddha land ever decline? The regions in the ten directions will all become treasure realms, and how could a treasure realm ever suffer harm? If you live in a country that knows no decline or

diminution, in a land that suffers no harm or disruption, then your body will find peace and security, and your mind will be calm and untroubled. You must believe my words; heed what I say! (WND-1, 25)

Excerpts from Ikeda Sensei's lecture in The Teachings for Victory, *vol. 7, pp. 160–63.*

Nichiren Daishonin's effort to "establish the correct teaching for the peace of the land" was a struggle against fundamental evil that rejects fundamental good—that is, rejects the attainment of enlightenment by all people.

In this section, speaking as the host, he sternly admonishes the guest to prevent him from falling prey to evil doctrines that entangle people in slander of the Law. Using such expressions as "the prison of these distorted doctrines," "the snares of these evil doctrines," and "this net of slanderous teachings," he employs the metaphors to stress how difficult it is to free oneself from slander of the Law.

The expression "lose their way in these mists and miasmas" likens confusion in this lifetime regarding the correct teaching of Buddhism to being enveloped in thick mist and haze. The "raging flames of hell" likens the agony of falling into the hell of incessant suffering to raging flames.

The Daishonin confidently teaches the way by which people can free themselves from the chains of misfortune and bring peace and security to society. It requires a transformation of the "tenets that we hold in our heart," he says, a fundamental revolution of our innermost state of mind.

What we have faith in indicates what we hold most precious, what values we cherish. It establishes our fundamental purpose and direction in life.

In other words, are we driven by egoism that seeks personal happiness at the exclusion and expense of others, or by compassion that is concerned with both our own and others' welfare, refusing to build our happiness on the misfortune of others? The focus is on the transformation of our minds, our hearts, our values. It is the human revolution in a single individual. Without that, "establishing the correct teaching for the peace of the land" cannot be achieved.

When we transform our hearts and minds, what tenet or ideal should we base them on? According to the Daishonin, it is "the one true vehicle, the single good doctrine." "The single good doctrine" here is the ultimate good taught in the Lotus Sutra—the principle that all people can bring forth their inherent Buddha nature and attain enlightenment.

In his copy of the Daishonin's writings, first Soka Gakkai president Tsunesaburo Makiguchi heavily underlined the words "embrace the one true vehicle, the single good doctrine [of the Lotus Sutra]." Dedicating one's life to the single good doctrine of the Lotus Sutra is the sure way to transform the karma of all humankind.

The Ultimate Aim of "Establishing the Correct Teaching"

I would now like to reconfirm the principle of establishing the correct teaching for the peace of the land.

"Establishing the correct teaching," first of all, depends upon the transformation of the heart and mind, an inner transformation at the individual level. It requires awakening to the fundamental good within us, establishing in our hearts the principles of respect for human dignity and life that are taught in the Lotus Sutra and making them the core of our life philosophy. Only through the actions of such awakened individuals can the teachings of the Lotus Sutra be established as the underlying and guiding principles of society.

And since the essence of "establishing the correct teaching" is to build a spiritual foundation for peace in society, it is only natural that we should join forces with like-minded individuals and organizations, and work together to protect the dignity of life and realize world peace. Our cause is not exclusionary.

The most crucial thing is to foster individuals dedicated to "establishing the correct teaching." When one individual takes action to apply this principle in real life, they can reorient those around them in the direction of good and peace. "Establishing the correct teaching" ultimately comes down to producing a steady stream of courageous individuals committed to this mission.

The "land" in "establishing the correct teaching for the peace of the land" means the land or realm where people dwell, while "the peace of the land" that is our goal means actualizing a Buddha land and building a realm of happiness and peace for all people. The term *land*, therefore, is not defined narrowly as the nation-state, nor is it restricted to any particular country.

All-Inclusiveness and Eternal Relevance

The essential meaning of "peace of the land" is the diametric opposite of nationalism. It is a concept of peace that is inclusive and open to the world. At the same time, it encompasses and is relevant to the future as well, because the Buddha land includes all Jambudvipa—the entire world—and will endure forever.

A Buddha land means a society in which the Buddhist spirit of respect for human beings and life is vital and alive. It is a world that values the ideal of realizing happiness for ourselves and others.

In this section, the Daishonin asserts that the threefold world—the real world in which we live—is a Buddha land and a treasure realm that will never decline or be destroyed. As long as the "treasures of the heart" of those who reside there are not destroyed, the land will become an enduring Buddha land.

"Establishing the correct teaching for the peace of the land" is the fundamental spirit of the Soka Gakkai's people-centered movement.

Mr. Makiguchi, who as an educator had embarked on a program

of educational reform based on his wish for the happiness of all children, was deeply impressed by "On Establishing the Correct Teaching for the Peace of the Land." It was, in fact, one of the main reasons why he decided to start practicing Nichiren Buddhism.

Based on his belief that the sole purpose for religion's existence is to work for the happiness of humanity and make the world a better place,[1] Mr. Makiguchi began to propagate Nichiren Buddhism openly and broadly throughout society. He stood up courageously during World War II, which he saw as the proper time to remonstrate with the Japanese militarist government of the day. Even though he went to prison as a result, he continued to fight for the happiness of the people up to the very end, ultimately dying for his beliefs.

Second Soka Gakkai president Josei Toda, fully prepared for a struggle with the devilish nature of authority, stood up alone in the devastated ruins of postwar Japan with the vow to rebuild the Soka Gakkai and the movement for kosen-rufu. When, at age nineteen, I had my own fateful first encounter with him at a discussion meeting in Kamata (in Tokyo's Ota Ward), he was giving a lecture on "On Establishing the Correct Teaching for the Peace of the Land."

"I want to eliminate all misery and suffering from the face of the earth!" Mr. Toda's lion's roar still resounds in my heart.

Based on the shared vow of mentor and disciple, the three founding Soka Gakkai presidents have all dedicated their lives to the struggle of "establishing the correct teaching for the peace of the land" for the sake of people's happiness and to free all from misery and suffering.

The name Soka, which emerged from discussions between Mr. Makiguchi and Mr. Toda, means "value creation." What kind of value, then, are we committed to creating?

I believe it can be summed up as empowering suffering individuals we encounter by encouraging them to base their lives on the sound philosophy of the Mystic Law in order to realize peace and security for all people and the world. Both the practice of "establishing the correct teaching" and the mission of actualizing the "peace of the land" are encompassed in this spirit of Soka, or value creation—a spirit that treasures each individual and is dedicated to one-to-one dialogue.

In that regard, I would like to declare for all to hear that the Soka Gakkai is the organization that has truly inherited and is faithfully carrying on the Daishonin's struggle of "establishing the correct teaching for the peace of the land" in the present day.

"The Real Aspect of the Gohonzon": Tapping the Infinite Benefit of the Gohonzon Through Faith

Never seek this Gohonzon outside yourself. The Gohonzon exists only within the mortal flesh of us ordinary people who embrace the Lotus Sutra and chant Nam-myoho-renge-kyo. The body is the palace of the ninth consciousness,[2] the unchanging reality that reigns over all of life's functions. To be endowed with the Ten Worlds means that all ten, without a single exception, exist in one world. Because of this it is called a mandala. Mandala is a Sanskrit word that is translated as "perfectly endowed" or "a cluster of blessings." This Gohonzon also is found only in the two characters for faith.[3] This is what the sutra means when it states that one can "gain entrance through faith alone."[4] (WND-1, 832)

Excerpts from Ikeda Sensei's lecture in The Teachings for Victory, *vol. 4, pp. 9–11.*

Nichinyo must have been extremely moved to learn that the Gohonzon Nichiren gave her was the Gohonzon that had been revealed for the first time in the Latter Day of the Law. But, then, he discloses an even more astonishing fact: "Never seek this Gohonzon outside yourself. The Gohonzon exists only within the mortal flesh of us ordinary people who embrace the Lotus Sutra and chant Nam-myoho-renge-kyo." He is saying that the Gohonzon does not exist outside us but within our own lives. Shifting the focus of faith and practice from the external to the internal was a dramatic change.

In Nichiren's day—and, in many cases, even today—we find a deeply rooted view: "We are but small, insignificant beings and the ultimate reality and eternal value lies somewhere outside of us, somewhere far away." Such a way of thinking is inextricably connected with belief in some otherworldly, supernatural power.

Nichiren Buddhism, however, rejects this idea completely. It teaches the true reality of life in which the eternal and ultimate Law is revealed in the physical beings of the ordinary people, living right here and now.

The term Buddha, after all, means "enlightened one." To what did the Buddha become enlightened? To that which should form the true basis of our life—namely, the Law and the true essence of our being. He awoke to the universal Law permeating all phenomena, which had previously been obscured by fundamental darkness.[5] He awoke to the greatness of each individual's life that is one and indivisible with that Law.

"The Gohonzon exists only within the mortal flesh of us ordinary people"—the real significance here is that the Gohonzon Nichiren inscribed functions is the means by which we can awaken to and call forth the Gohonzon (the Buddhahood) within us. The physical Gohonzon we chant to is the very same Gohonzon that is in our heart; it is by chanting Nam-myoho-renge-kyo for the happiness of ourselves and others that we can clearly awaken to the Gohonzon within us.

In another letter to Nichinyo, he writes in a similar vein, "When I ponder where this 'Treasure Tower' chapter is now, I see that it exists in the eight-petaled lotus flower of the heart[6] within the breast of Nichinyo" ("The 'Entrustment' and Other Chapters," WND-1, 915). Both "within the mortal flesh" and "in the eight-petaled lotus flower of the heart" mean "within the depths of one's own life."

Still another way Nichiren describes our inner being is "the palace of the ninth consciousness, the unchanging reality that reigns over all of life's functions" ("The Real Aspect of the Gohonzon," WND-1, 832). The ninth consciousness—also the amala-consciousness, or pure consciousness—is often referred to in Buddhist texts as the "mind king"[7] or "ruler of the mind," indicating the fundamental entity of the mind itself. "The unchanging reality" means the ultimate truth, free from all delusion. Since the "mind king" dwells in this unchanging reality, our mortal bodies are called its "palace."

In "Reply to Kyo'o," the Daishonin writes, "I, Nichiren, have inscribed my life in sumi ink, so believe in the Gohonzon with your whole heart" (WND-1, 412). He is saying here that he has inscribed in the form of the Gohonzon the life state of Buddhahood that he has attained as a votary of the Lotus Sutra, a life state that is identical with the unchanging reality.

The Gohonzon is in the form of a mandala. The Sanskrit term mandala has also been translated into Chinese as "perfectly endowed" and "a cluster of blessings" (see "The Real Aspect of the Gohonzon," WND-1, 832). It means a trove of infinite benefit that we can draw from and enjoy freely.

Mr. Toda said, "Nichiren Daishonin's life is Nam-myoho-renge-kyo, so our lives, as his disciples, are also Nam-myoho-renge-kyo."[8] On another occasion, he declared: "When we embrace faith in the Mystic Law, the fundamental power of Nichiren Daishonin wells up in response from within our beings, and we, too, reveal our true self—that is, our true enlightened nature that is one with the eternal, unchanging reality."[9]

Attaining Immeasurable Benefit by "Gaining Entrance Through Faith Alone"

Nichiren further explains: "This Gohonzon also is found only in the two characters for faith. This is what the sutra means when it states that one can 'gain entrance through faith alone'" ("The Real Aspect of the Gohonzon," WND-1, 832). Faith, in a word, is the key to attaining Buddhahood. Even Shariputra, who was known as foremost in wisdom among Shakyamuni's disciples, gained entrance into the ultimate truth of the Lotus Sutra through faith. This is the meaning of the Lotus Sutra passage "to gain entrance through faith alone."

When we ordinary people of the Latter Day face the Gohonzon, the embodiment of the boundless life state of Buddhahood, and chant Nam-myoho-renge-kyo with deep and strong faith, we can gain entrance to the shining realm of time without beginning manifested in the Gohonzon. Nichiren refers to the Gohonzon as the "object of devotion for observing the mind." The purpose of the Gohonzon is to enable us to "observe our mind," that is, to see and awaken to the Buddhahood within our own lives. But being able to see the true nature of our mind, or attain enlightenment, is not something achieved through conceptual thought or meditative practice; faith is the foundation. That is why, he writes, "This Gohonzon also is found only in the two characters for faith." The "object of devotion for observing the mind" is the "object of devotion of faith."

The Gohonzon (Buddhahood) manifests in the lives of those who have strong faith. A person may possess the Gohonzon, but without faith, they will receive no benefit. Faith is what causes the "cluster of blessings" that is the Gohonzon to manifest in our lives. Accordingly, as long as our faith stays alive, the "cluster of blessings" will never disappear. Even if we were to lose our physical Gohonzon in an accident or natural disaster, as long as we retain our faith, the Gohonzon within our lives remain intact and we can activate its beneficial power.

Only when we have faith does the beneficial power of the Gohonzon manifest itself. Truly, the Gohonzon is found in our faith alone.

NOTES:

1. Translated from Japanese. See Tsunesaburo Makiguchi, *Soka kyoiku-gaku taikei* [The system of value-creating education] in *Makiguchi Tsunesaburo zenshu* [The collected writings of Tsunesaburo Makiguchi], vol. 5 (Tokyo: Daisanbunmei-sha, 2005), 356.

2. Ninth consciousness: Also, *amala*-consciousness. The Buddha nature, or the fundamental purifying force, that is free from all karmic impediments. Here, the Daishonin is associating it with Nam-myoho-renge-kyo.

3. The Japanese word *faith* consists of two Chinese characters.

4. *The Lotus Sutra and Its Opening and Closing Sutras*, trans. Burton Watson (Tokyo: Soka Gakkai, 2009), 110.

5. Fundamental darkness, or fundamental ignorance: The most deeply rooted illusion inherent in life, said to give rise to all other illusions. The inability to see or recognize the truth, particularly, the true nature of one's life.

6. The "eight-petaled lotus flower of the heart" refers to the arrangement of the heart, lungs, and other organs in the chest cavity, which was thought to resemble an eight-petaled lotus blossom.

7. The "mind king" refers to the core of the mind, which controls the various workings of the mind.

8. Translated from Japanese. Josei Toda, *Toda Josei zenshu* [The collected writings of Josei Toda], vol. 5 (Tokyo: Seikyo Shimbun-sha, 1985), 271.

9. Translated from Japanese. Josei Toda, *Toda Josei zenshu* [The collected writings of Josei Toda], vol. 2 (Tokyo: Seikyo Shimbun-sha, 1992), 11.